OFFICE LADIES FACTORY WOMEN

LIFE AND WORK AT
A JAPANESE COMPANY

JEANNIE LO

An East Gate Book

M. E. Sharpe, Inc.
Armonk, New York
London, England

An East Gate Book

Copyright © 1990 by M. E. Sharpe, Inc.

Library of Congress Cataloging-in-Publication Data

Lo, Jeannie, 1965–
Office ladies/factory women : life and work at a Japanese company
/ by Jeannie Lo.
p. cm.
ISBN 0-87332-598-2 (c); ISBN 0-87332-599-0 (p)
Includes index.
1. Women—Employment—Japan—Case studies.
2. Burazā Kōgyō Kabushiki Kaisha—Employees.
I. Title
HD6197.L6   1990
331.4′0952—dc20
89-70365
CIP

ED (c)   10   9   8   7   6   5   4   3   2   1

ED (p)   10   9   8   7   6   5   4   3   2   1

Contents

ACKNOWLEDGMENTS

THIS WORK could not have been realized without the participation of many. I am extremely grateful to the Harvard University Reischauer Institute and the Radcliffe College Murray Fellowships Committee for sponsoring my research. I am grateful to the management and employees of Brother for allowing me to do research at their company, for listening to all of my requests, and for their hospitality and friendship. I thank my many advisers, including professors Ronald Dore, Merry White, Susan Pharr, and Ezra Vogel. I am indebted to Hugh Shapiro and Professor William D. Johnston for expert editorial advice, and to Professor Shunsuke Nagashima of Nara Women's College for his informative discussions. I thank Richard L. Meyer for helping with the final preparations.

The names that appear in this book have been changed to protect the privacy of the informants.

CHAPTER ONE

Arriving in Japan

THE CHANCE to go to Japan came when the telephone rang in my Harvard dormitory room one lazy morning in April 1986, waking me from an unintended nap. On the phone was Bill Johnston, my junior-year East Asian Studies tutorial section leader, who asked me if I wanted to spend the summer working in a Japanese company. This was how everything began.

By May all of the arrangements had been made. I would be a translator, proofreader, and English teacher for Brother Industries in Nagoya, Japan. Things were not quite settled on the Japanese side, my liaison at Brother International, New Jersey, told me. The management at Brother in Nagoya had wanted a male intern from Harvard; I was a young Asian woman. Many of the Japanese speculated that I would get homesick. Yoshino and Kaneko, two women who worked in the education section of the Brother Industries personnel division, later remarked, ''Men are independent, but women get homesick.'' After some deliberation, however, the directors at Brother agreed to accept me as their first office lady (OL) from the United States.

I came to understand what it means to be an OL, a woman who works in an office in Japan. Brother hires OLs to assume a wide range of responsibilities. The offices bustle with the activities of these women and the salarymen. Unlike American-style offices,

3

Brother offices have no partitions, and the entire workplace unit—
the OLs, salarymen, management—congregates and conducts business within a single room. My desk was one in a neat cluster of
desks of three OLs, about ten feet away from Iwata, my section
chief. This gave me a great vantage point for observing the lives
and dealings in a Japanese office. I saw young women run off to
the kitchen to prepare coffee and green tea and do the dishes. I saw
them wait tirelessly by the facsimile and copy machines while the
younger salarymen remained hunched over their desks, pushing
numbers and doing columns of calculations. The bosses came in
and out, as they were usually on business trips or making deals and
interacting with customers all over the country. When I sat at my
desk, members of the planning office could also watch me; I gauged
their reactions to the various things that I did. As an OL in this group,
with my desk firmly planted in the formal structure of the office, I
was allowed to participate in all of its social activities, company
planned or not.

I was housed in Aoi dormitory, the Brother dormitory for single
female workers, where I met and talked with many different female
employees whom I would not have known otherwise. I played on
the company women's rugby team, the Brother Hangovers. This
team represented the city of Nagoya and had a membership of
Brother employees and female athletes from Aichi Prefecture.
Gaining acceptance into these exclusive groups taught me much
about the structure of Japanese society and the difficulties of doing
field research in Japan.

I stayed on as an OL in the Brother Sales Company until the
first week of November 1986. I became a researcher in the
Brother Life Research Center of the Brother Industries Marketing
Research Group. At the LRC I studied the topic that I was interested in—Japanese women in the company. My subjects were
218 female workers at Brother Industries and Brother Sales. My
work there inspired me to look at another group of workers—
those in the factory.

I returned to the United States in February 1987 to begin my senior year at Harvard. I tried to read up on Japanese women's issues in the available English and Japanese sources but found little written on the subject. Scholars and researchers on contemporary Japan bemoan the sparseness of literature on the modern Japanese woman. There are many scattered sources, a hodgepodge of newspaper articles, insurance company surveys, and government white papers on working women, but the information presented is inadequate. There is little discussion on how Japanese working women spend their daily lives, what motivates them, and what inhibits them. Yet I was determined to go through the available sources with a fine-toothed comb to pick out relevant details. In the more than two hundred hours I spent on this project, I found that the scope of the Japanese newspaper articles was extremely limited. The articles from 1985 and 1986 focused on the employment dilemmas of female university graduates, but not of graduates of junior colleges, high schools, or vocational schools. Editorial boards of Japanese magazines chose as their topics other kinds of female workers: Tokyo women in management, and career women in the ''katakana'' professions. Katakana is a Japanese phonetic system used to express words borrowed from other languages. Individuals in katakana professions—interior designers, stewardesses, editors, engineers—have careers whose job descriptions were created after Japan internationalized and built highly competitive industries in the 1960s. Job titles for such careers are in English.

The paucity of literature on female labor in Japan encouraged me to return to Brother Industries, this time as an on-line factory woman. I wanted to understand factory women using two different approaches: first, I would live in their environment and follow the movements of their daily lives; then I would interview them and listen to their stories and reflections on life and work. Officials in the personnel department gave me special permission to join the home typewriter production line at the Mizuho plant. Working on the assembly line, I could take notes on daily conversations. I lived with the women and shared what I believed were pain and joys similar to theirs. Although fieldwork in the factory was much more taxing physically and mentally than my experiences in the planning office, I found it equally rewarding.

Without having experienced the lives of factory women and office ladies, I would not have been able to understand the differences. As a factory woman, I worked inside a large plant composed of gray buildings filled with automated lines of green machines that regulated the flow of manufacture and filled the air with deafening noises of parts being manipulated, shaped, aligned, screwed in, and greased. During a typical day at the plant, long lines of young female workers stood for hours at their assigned spots, working intently, busily threading wires, adjusting screws, and keeping up with their female companions on the line. Although the women were tired and their hands and bodies smelled of black grease, the click-clacking of the machines in the background helped keep them going by reinforcing the pace and rhythm of their work. It permeated their minds and implored steadiness.

I immersed myself in the lives of my subjects. More than just an observer or interviewer, I became part of the Nagoya workplace. Informants became friends, and Nagoya and Brother became a second home to me. Spending time with the families of many women in my various workplaces, and staying up late to watch television and talk to factory women and OLs in the dormitory, gave me an understanding of their lives and motivations only dimly perceived from my preliminary questionnaire, interviews, or time spent in the office or on the line.

In this book, I explain the roles of female workers in the office and factory, and the ways they view their lives and work. I examine how OLs and factory women form and maintain work and social relationships, and I consider their reasons for working, levels of ambition, and actions and expectations. By living with both office ladies and factory women, I was able to compare them, their lifestyles, and their concerns.

Any documentation of the contemporary woman laborer must be prefaced by discussion of the historical development of female roles in Japanese labor. Attitudes toward women today have their origins in upper-caste Tokugawa views of women's position in society. The woman's role in the landowner class was that of homemaker and bearer of children. Every child had a specific function in the family, dictated by gender and order of birth. Parents invested the survival of the family in the hands of the eldest son, who inherited the family fortune and lands. All other sons and daughters were a drain on the family savings. Daughters were the least valued of the children. Female infanticide in the form of *mabiki* (thinning) was a common practice justified by the economic survival of the family (Taeuber 1958, 29). Families hoped to marry off their surviving daughters at an early age; fewer dependents meant more food per person.

During the Meiji period women left their homes to work on farms or in factories, or to be sold into houses of prostitution. Many of these women sent their wages home to lighten family economic burdens. Their absence alone, by decreasing the number of mouths to feed, increased the chances for survival of the family. Not living at home, young unmarried women were no longer dependents or *gokutsubushi*, literally "grain wasters," a derisive term for children and other relatives who drained family resources by eating and not working to replenish the food stores. Many women were sold into slavery or prostitution and never returned to see their families again.

Industrialization opened up new opportunities for young unmarried women. From the early Meiji period (1868–1912), both *mabiki* and indenturing young daughters into prostitution became rare. The emergence of factories and textile mills created new jobs for women. Meiji leaders regarded Japan's young daughters as the country's greatest natural resource. Like the developed nations of Europe and the United States, Japan also boasted a large female work force that labored under poor conditions for low wages

(Sievers 1983, 56). Yet Meiji industrialization had little effect on the traditional views of women's status.

The diversification of female labor occurred in later years. This was a slow process, since even up to 1945, most Japanese believed that a woman's primary function was reproduction. This accounted for the Japanese reluctance to use women in army matériel factories during World War II (Havens 1975, 920). Following the U.S. occupation, Japanese industry modernized and grew rapidly. The 1960s were a time of heightened international contact and awareness—largely a result of the 1964 Olympics in Tokyo, which brought many visitors to Japan. The new Tokyo bullet train bridged the great distance between Tokyo and Osaka, the two largest cities, enabling commuters to travel between the two cities in three hours. Mom-and-pop stores began to disappear as the industrial giants took over. Large-scale migration settled one-quarter of the Japanese population in cities between Tokyo and Osaka by 1972.

New demands arose with urbanization. Companies were built to meet communications and consumer needs of the new age. High-tech industries produced computers, typewriters, stereos, word processors, televisions, and other media products. The expansion of factories led in turn to the growth in the number and diversity of jobs for women. OLs helped to organize operations for selling new products, which factory women assembled. The structure of industries in the 1980s, and the roles that women play within that structure, are products of postwar industrialization.

Although the content of office jobs changed as small companies evolved into large-scale industries, the upper-caste Tokugawa idea that women should perform domestic tasks to support the lifestyles of men remains. OLs in the 1980s still perform secondary or domestic functions in the office. Besides their projects in the office and clerical work, they are responsible for domestic and traditionally female tasks. OLs become instructors, office housekeepers, and hostesses, serving tea to the men in their work group and to company clients.

The number of factory jobs in high-tech industries in the 1960s rose concurrently with the increase in the number of OLs and salarymen. Japanese companies such as Brother hired many women for on-line assembly work, since they were a cheap form of labor and usually left the company within a few years to make way for a new crop of low-paid women workers. Women rarely gained the seniority that would merit high wages; they were also paid less than men because they usually had less education. Japanese parents tend to be more supportive of male education than female education.

For the most part, females in industrialized Japan make life decisions that conform to social expectations. They work in companies as either OLs or factory workers after graduating from junior high school, high school, or junior college. Their positions depend greatly upon their level of education: junior high school graduates become factory women, while college-educated women take OL positions; high school graduates become either. Women work in their assigned work groups for several years, until they marry or have children and quit because of family or society's expectations.

Male and female roles are clearly defined in Japanese society. Only a woman can be the *sengyo shufu*, or professional housewife—that is, a housewife should view her role as a profession, a job to which she must devote all of her time. The concept of shared roles is inconceivable. This stems from the idea that women—not men—are responsible for raising the children. Women who choose to work rather than devote their energies to their children are thought to be "bad mothers." Merry White, in *The Japanese Educational Challenge* (1986, 13), describes the amount of time and attention given to a child's education: "Mothers are intensely committed to their children from the onset of pregnancy and see their major life's task as the rearing of successful children. Mothers are always looking for innovative ways to enhance their children's life chances."

White-collar workers in the administrative offices of Brother

Industries voiced similar opinions. One twenty-four-year-old salaryman said, "It's bad enough to have a wife who neglects her housework and husband by pursuing a career, but a mother who dashes her child's hopes of entering Tokyo or Keio University or any other prestigious institution of higher learning [and, in effect, destroying his chances for a successful future] is unthinkable." Japanese mothers exert great influence on the education and social well-being of their children. The specific roles of women in society dictate that a woman must commit all of her time and energy to her family.

Nevertheless, there have been many changes in the profile of female labor since 1945. The turnover rates for Japanese female labor have decreased, for example. In 1949, the average age of female workers was 23.8. In 1970, it rose to 29.8, and then to 34.9 in 1980 (Robins-Mowry 1983, 168). This rise in the average age of working women can be accounted for in part by the increasing number of women in their forties and fifties who reenter the work force when their children have gone off to college and no longer need their care. Some 24.9 million women were in the labor force in Japan in 1987, accounting for 39.9 percent of the entire Japanese work force—a percentage that has risen annually since 1975. Now approximately 66 percent of all Japanese female workers are married, an increase over the 62.1 percent figure of 1975.

The structure of the female work force has also changed in recent years because of the aging of the population. A drop in the percentage of women in their twenties has been accompanied by an increase in the number of women thirty-five years old and older, who accounted for 58.8 percent of Japan's female workers in 1987.

The average number of years that a woman works in a company has grown from 3.2 in 1950 to 6.9 in 1979 (Robins-Mowry 1983, 169). Women's wages have risen slowly since 1958. Their salaries in 1985 were reported to be 51.8 percent of men's wages (Statistics Bureau 1986).

The 1986 labor force profiles of Brother are different from those of the country overall. The average age of this company's workers is twenty-five. (Brother employs few older women who come back to work after their children are in college.) There are approximately two thousand women in the company's labor force. The turnover rate for workers is high. Most women enter the company after graduating from high school or college and leave within five years to marry or for other reasons. Salaries at Brother are determined by employees' educational level and seniority. In part, this explains the large number of women factory workers. Women's salaries remain low because most women do not achieve more than five years of seniority. Brother hires many more women than men for its blue-collar labor force because women's salaries tend to be lower.

The idea of hiring cheap labor is not so important when it comes to office workers. Experience and training are essential for the financial success of the company. Offices depend more on college-educated men than on OLs, the cheaper form of labor. The ratio of salarymen to OLs is more balanced than the male-female ratio in the factories. The distribution of responsibility in the offices is far from equal, however. Salarymen make all of the major decisions in the company. The OLs provide support by performing secretarial, housekeeping, or hostess duties. Many of the men in the company will move on to managerial positions, but OLs are rarely promoted: company policies bar women from management.

In doing research for this book, I probed the views of work and life ambitions of both OLs and factory women through interviews and questionnaires. In the following pages I examine the internal hierarchies of the office and factory and discuss ways in which the structure of workplace relationships and social customs inform perceptions of work, lifestyle, motivations, and ambitions of women workers.

Marriage is a key social phenomenon examined in this work. Many Japanese whom I interviewed believe that marriage is part of the natural progression from the impulsiveness of adolescence to the stability of responsible adulthood. For them, marriage is a stabilizing institution. Men who are not married by age thirty are encouraged to do so for reasons of mental balance. Marriage pushes young men and women onto the next plateau of maturity. It forces salarymen to leave the confines of the single men's dormitories, where they play mahjong and carouse with their colleagues from work, and puts an unceremonious end to their recreational lives by heaping new financial responsibilities on them. Young married men no longer have to do their own laundry, but they must support a wife and a family, make house payments, and act in a manner befitting a mature adult.

Marriage is also believed to be a stabilizing influence on women. By marrying, a woman fulfills a basic social commitment to her family. She leaves her home to live with her husband, and in some cases with her in-laws too. Her dependence on the family she grew up in is transferred to her husband's family. Through this transfer, she fulfills a basic purpose in her life, her "goal in." Marriage is a goal for young people. A person who marries gets his or her life goal in and scores points in maturity.

For some women, however, marriage is a progression from independent working life to the comfortable dependency of home life. By marrying a salaryman, a woman can quit her job and devote herself to managing a household. Marriage, for most, is a means of escape from the tedium of factory work, unchallenging OL responsibilities, and the paternalism of single women's dormitories.

Marriage in Japan is not only a social commitment but also an economic one. Traditional marriage customs hold that the man must give his fiancée a *yuino* or special engagement present (Hendry 1981, 156). This customary gift usually consists of 500,000 yen ($4,000) and an expensive diamond engagement ring. Japanese jewelry companies have managed, with a massive advertising campaign, to set the convention for the cost of the ring. One such advertisement in the October 1987 issue of *With*, a Japanese women's monthly, states: "On your ring finger, a diamond engagement ring of three months' [salary].'' The size and quality of the diamond are good indicators of the husband's income and social status.

In return, the woman traditionally gives her fiancé an elaborate dowry consisting of several truckloads of furniture, expensive handmade silk kimonos, and other items to be used in the married household. Now, however, many young people give each other only small gifts and save their money to finance the exorbitant costs of the wedding ceremony and honeymoon. In 1986, the average cost of Japanese wedding packages (including the ceremony and a week-long honeymoon in Hawaii) amounted to approximately 700,000 yen ($50,000). Nagoya prides itself on having the most expensive wedding packages in Japan. It is reputedly Japan's most conservative city, where people still practice age-old marriage customs.

The expense of marriage is so great that even planning for marriage requires maturity. One cannot marry on impulse. Marriage is a well-thought-out process that "stabilizes" the lifestyle of an individual and involves considerable financial planning and saving. For Japanese women, work is the means to marriage. After graduating from school, women labor in factories and offices to save the hundreds of thousands of yen necessary for the rituals of marriage, and they supplement these savings with loans from their parents. Essentially women work to pay for their dowries, for their living and entertainment expenses as single women, and for travel. Once married, they achieve financial security and are dependent on their husbands rather than on their fathers or companies.

Other forces that influence the work attitudes of the office ladies and factory women are the content and structure of their work relationships. There are many kinds of ties: the worker-boss relationship in which the OL or factory woman follows the directions of her designated superiors; the senior-junior ties in which younger workers depend on senior workers as instructors and advisers; colleague affinities; and paternalistic bonds between women and company officials inherent in the structure of the dormitory. These relationships are analyzed here in the context of the workplace and the dormitory to answer the questions: How do women at Brother view their working lives, and how is this perception informed by company practices?

In chapter five I compare the office lady and factory woman in terms of how they fit into the company structure and how their positions in this network influence their perceptions of work and life. Both types of worker—like all women in Japan—are subject to the same pressures to marry and have children. It will become clear, however, that the differences between the way the company treats OLs and factory women account for discrepancies in their lifestyles and the way they think about work.

Nagoya, Japan's third largest city, is the home of Brother Industries. The area is in some respects idiosyncratic. Many Japanese assert that Japan is a homogeneous island country with a common language and culture. Yet a one-hour ride on the train from the Kanto to the Kansai region reveals a world of difference between the people in Tokyo and those in Osaka. Even more than the other large cities in Japan, Nagoya maintains traditional values and, outside of the small business and commercial neighborhood of Sakae, a rural atmosphere.

Labeled "Japan's biggest *inaka*" (rural area, implying a lack of culture), Nagoya is also the most conservative city in Japan. This reputation comes from the indigenous culture, which is quite different from that of other Japanese cities. Nagoya's residents retain certain preferences. They prefer, for example, red miso soup while the rest of the country enjoys white or mixed miso soup. They have many indigenous dishes and ways of speaking. Japanese in other regions label the Nagoya dialect a "dirty" one because it has many nasal tones, and the language is the butt of many comedians' jokes throughout the nation. The local fashion sense is different; the summer I spent there was one in which Nagoya women raved about polka-dots, popular only in their city.

Yet more than these obvious differences in taste, the culture of Nagoya shows a distinct reluctance to depart from past rituals. Many still practice the customs of dowries and engagement gifts. The conservative views of marriage are reflected in Brother policies on women workers.

Aichi Prefecture has many industries. It is home to the Toyota Motor Company; to Inax, the maker of ceramic tiles and bathroom fixtures; and to Brother, a producer of typewriters, word processors, facsimile machines, and sewing machines for export and domestic sale. Factories, office buildings, and concrete high-rises line the streets of Nagoya. Some sections of the city, including the part where Brother Industries is located and the downtown sections, were left untouched during the bombings of World War II and retain an ancient mien. There are two major shopping districts and one red-light district where salarymen go to forget the stresses of work in the company of young bar hostesses and company cohorts, and drown their tensions in glasses of beer, sake, and whiskey.

The physical structures of Nagoya are like those in any other Japanese city, with a single difference: Brother permeates the city. It is difficult to walk down the streets without meeting Brother employees or seeing Brother signs, factories, or billboards advertising Brother products. The company, which employs five thousand workers and is considered to be on the small end of the grouping of large industries of Japan, built its headquarters in Horita, in a small section of Mizuho Ward, about fifty years ago. The factory and one of the offices where I worked are located next to company headquarters.

I found it convenient to do research in Horita. I taught English to office and factory workers and made friends in those communities. Living in Horita for ten months, I became familiar with local faces and shops and involved in the community. I also came to understand the basic structure of Japanese companies, of which Brother is a good example. A new employee chooses the company, not the job. Brother employees are assigned their posts—factory worker, janitor, executive secretary—after they are hired, and they usually have little say in the process.

I analyzed company regulations and culture and their impact on women workers using three different methodologies: fieldwork, interviews, and a questionnaire. Each method has its advantages and pitfalls. The questionnaire allowed me to examine the opinions of 218 women employees but did not give me specific information on individuals. Interviews of a select group of individuals supplemented the questionnaire, and fieldwork put me in their shoes and gave me hands-on experience building typewriters and working in an office. Being Asian, I was able to immerse myself into the culture and the Asian environment and be a less conspicuous participant than a non-Asian would have been.

There are many difficulties that arise when one sets out to compare office ladies and factory women. One is singling out prototypes for study. There are marked differences between individuals, resulting from diverse ages, birthplaces, personal and social backgrounds, and a myriad of other factors. Many times the observer cannot tell which factors have the greatest effect on the subject. What follows, then, is a study of selected women in one company in a traditional Japanese city.

CHAPTER TWO

A Day in the Factory

THE DAY for factory women begins around 6:00 A.M., or perhaps a bit earlier if they have been assigned to early morning cleanup duties in the company women's dormitory. Women who commute from the far reaches of Aichi Prefecture must start even earlier.

Summers in Nagoya are so unbearably hot that many dorm residents leave the door to their room open to let a breeze in through the sliding doors off the veranda, and they sleep in the main room instead of the tiny, cramped bedroom. With my door open, I woke up at 6:00 sharp every morning to the voices of the sweepers outside my door and the sounds of women cleaning the toilets.

By 6:05 I was up. I turned on the television set to listen to the weather report while I washed my face. When I did laundry in the morning I got up much earlier and rushed to the laundry room with a load in my arms. I usually met bright-eyed dormmates chattering away on the weather or work as they did their ironing or their laundry. The dormitory head always came minutes before 6:00 to open the doors to the laundry rooms and kitchens. Of the six washing machines, five were rather primitive tubs that merely spun the clothes around. The clothes had to be removed and wrung out in a side compartment after each wash or rinse. I later discovered that this type of washing machine is typical in Japan, despite the fact that many households are now investing in ''American-style''

17

large automatics. There was one automatic machine in the dorm, but no one used it because it did not work very well and left a soapy film on the clothes.

Laundry was an ordeal. The machines were small and could wash only about six articles of clothing at a time, so the women ended up doing laundry three days a week. It took about forty-five minutes to do the wash. Then we had to hang the wet clothes on clotheslines to dry. Laundry is considered women's work. The men's dormitories, in contrast, are equipped with working automatic washing machines on every floor, saving time and effort. By the time I finished my laundry, it was usually 7:00. Running back and forth between my room and the laundry room, I took some time out to boil water for tea and iron the Brother uniform that had been lent to me.

At 7:00 I went to breakfast with many of the other girls in the dormitory. The breakfast menu was not terribly exciting. Since the opening of the Aoi dormitory doors to women employees in 1980, the cafeteria maids have served a set breakfast of rice, a small packet of flavored *nori* seaweed, white miso soup, pickled turnips, and low-grade green tea. The exceptions were Tuesdays, when we were allowed a raw egg to put into our rice, and Sundays, when we ate the dormitory's version of a Western breakfast: one slice of buttered toast and some green tea.

Microwaves in the rear of the dining room were an added convenience. Women who did not enjoy raw eggs could microwave them. People were also allowed to buy food outside of the dormitory and prepare it in these ovens. To save money, some did not go to the dining hall in the morning but made breakfasts of boiled noodles in the tiny kitchens on their floor or in the large kitchen on the first floor, or ate bread in the factory dining hall before the loudspeaker sounded for the lines to start up.

In any case, breakfast at the dormitory was not very social. Most women wandered in alone or with one other person, ate breakfast quickly, and then left for their rooms to change into their work clothes. Certain groups did eat together, though. Women on company athletic teams joined for breakfast promptly at 6:00 when the dining halls opened. They ate the general fare plus a special diet of yogurt and other foods that would help their performance in practices. They also got a raw egg from the dining hall every morning. These women always sat together, with the younger workers bringing the food and serving it to the senior workers. The team kept its own refrigerator in the dining room, stocked with fruit, dairy products, and meat or fish to flavor the rice. The women cut their hair short and often poked each other in the ribs, laughing and telling one another that they looked like "handsome young men." Yet they carried themselves with pride. The other employees respected them and expressed no jealousy. A factory woman living in the dormitory explained, "The handball players work very hard in their practices and games. They deserve the special treatment."

The rest of the female workers came downstairs to the dining hall in waves. The second rush of people came at 6:30. They were the early risers, the women chosen to do that morning's dormitory chores, and the factory women. The plant started up at 8:00, but the downtown offices (in the center of Nagoya) opened at 9:00. The third group came in between 7:00 and 8:00. These were team members who had to jog or do special training exercises before breakfast. The joggers ate quickly and were allowed a quick shower before going off to their jobs.

After breakfast, we returned to our rooms and changed into uniforms. Then we went to the reception area in front of the dormitory management's office and turned our nameplates, hanging on a big board on the wall, from the black-lettered side over to the red-lettered side, indicating that we had left the dormitory for the day. We left through a side door into the foyer lined with rows of numbered boxes. There we traded our dormitory slippers for street shoes. This foyer served as a midway point between the reception area and the outside world. The factory women changed into comfortable cloth shoes to work on the line while the OLs changed into heeled pumps or other leather shoes. The factory was a seven-minute walk from the dormitory. The women usually left by 7:40. At the front entrance off Horita Street the guard who sat by the gate smiled widely and bowed a friendly ''Good morning'' to the workers who passed into the faded concrete building. Brother has many different plants throughout Aichi Prefecture and Japan; the one at the Mizuho complex consists of eight weather-worn gray glass and concrete buildings. The workers inside these structures build typewriters, word processors, and sewing machines, products that are immediately packed up and shipped to many different parts of the world.

The workers entered the plant and walked to their designated areas. By 7:50 the locker rooms were filled with young women and men. The men's locker room was on the first floor in the first room off the main entrance. Women working on the typewriter and word processor lines used the locker room on the third floor, off a semiprivate hallway away from the lines. The lockers were a personal space for the workers, filled with each person's belongings. Many women left makeup cases and boxed lunches there until lunchtime. Some factory women spent the early morning, part of their lunch hour, and late afternoon after work at their lockers touching up their faces to look their best for factory work or for a date.

Men and women who had commuted to work changed into their company uniforms: men into tan cotton shirts and pants and women into blue polyester-blend skirts and shirts with the company logo sewn onto the sleeves. The uniforms for the women look like airline stewardess uniforms from the 1950s, or the ''uniforms worn by female gas station attendants,'' in the words of the woman whose locker was next to mine. They are actually an improvement over the solid blue polyester skirts and shirts worn five years ago. Many of the young OLs wore the shirts tucked into their skirts to accentuate their figure; the older ones, more modest, wore less makeup and their shirts out of their skirts.

The locker rooms buzzed with gossip and small talk about daily lives, about what a coworker was planning to do on the weekend or who she was dating, or about whether mandatory overtime work would be imposed that day. Some high school girls who did part-time work in the factory during their summer vacations came in their school uniforms—navy-blue sailor suit dresses. The factory was short about a hundred workers and had resorted to hiring students on summer vacation for part-time labor.

After changing, some women hurried off to the cafeteria for a quick cup of coffee before beginning work. Others walked leisurely to their workplaces to sit and relax for five minutes before beginning another tiring day on the line. At 7:55, the music for stretching and the morning exercises played over the loudspeaker. The popular program known as ''radio exercise'' has been broadcast every morning since the 1930s without fail. A woman's voice counts off the exercises in clear Japanese in the foreground of bright music. At Brother, the older men stood and stretched their flanks, arms, and back muscles, twisting and turning their torsos. They started their day the same way every morning, setting into motion the muscles that they used to lift the packages onto trucks day after day. These men smiled and stretched as they brushed off the remnants of morning weariness and bade hello to the people entering the workplace. Sometimes the young engineers found exercise time all too amusing and just flapped their arms and gawked at passersby.

The young women who worked on the lines were indifferent to

the music, and none of them did the stretching. The stragglers were changing; the rest spent their last minutes of freedom adjusting their hair and makeup, or drinking their coffee. Most people were positioned on the line about one or two minutes before the work began. They ate candy and gossiped. Early morning was a very social time. At 7:59 A.M., a recording of church bells sounded over the public address system; with the chimes, the workday began.

There were four lines in operation on my floor: a robot line and three "human" lines. The robot line made two thousand typewriter bodies a day. The robots worked tirelessly, 24 hours a day, 7 days a week, 365 days a year, and were highly efficient. There was one male engineer who inspected this line regularly and stood by to ensure that there were no breakdowns. The products of the robot line were then sent over to three human lines: a main line, a subline, and an office typewriter line. The human lines, less than perfect in comparison, worked only eight to nine hours a day and did all of the simple motions that required judgment, like spreading grease, inserting springs, applying labels, and testing machine functions. I was assigned to the subline.

Although mass production usually began exactly at 8:00, it was delayed some mornings for five or ten minutes. One of the managers, Iwasaki, gave pep talks on Mondays and Tuesdays. We stood on the line, next to our workbenches, facing him. He seemed to hope that the cheer he spread would foster a greater sense of loyalty to the group and result in higher productivity for the rest of the week. He usually began by relating the news of the company. In one speech, Iwasaki talked about a companywide athletic competition in a nearby prefecture, some engineers who were visiting from the United Kingdom, and finally about sticking it out on the line and giving our "100 percent." Some of the women on the line looked indifferent to his appeals, averting their eyes and staring at the floor as he spoke, but others listened attentively and smiled in appreciation. They were ready to begin work. Iwasaki radiated a paternal message with his kind words. He was a soft-spoken man who seemed to be concerned with our well-being. He stressed the importance of safety and teamwork, restating the message of the "safety first" signs that were posted by all of the elevators and on the factory walls. Iwasaki beamed: he was silently yet unmistakably proud of the women on the line. What this meant to them, I did not know for sure.

His speech ended at 8:10. The women were silent throughout it and remained so afterward. We then put on our white cotton gloves, which were a testimony of the kind of work we did on the line. (Within three hours, our gloves were perforated, and completely soiled with black grease. We covered the parts of the gloves where the fingers poked through with cotton finger replacements.) When we finished putting our gloves on, Tomita, one of the two senior workers responsible for our group's production, turned on the loading machine at the beginning of the line. The machine loaded one typewriter chassis onto the line every twenty seconds and emitted a loud BUZZ! at the end of each of these intervals to tell us that we should be starting on the next typewriter. There were now typewriters in various stages of manufacture down the line. Tomita yelled down the line to tell all that work had begun: "It's going!"

We immediately began to work on the typewriter body in front of us. Many of the women on the line had built Brother typewriters for over a year. Their duties in the typewriter manufacturing process had become second nature to them. Typewriter models varied from year to year, but the motions performed on the line did not change significantly. The senior workers guided the junior workers through the small changes in procedure. But most of the women ended up doing the same kind of work as before. During the summer of 1987, we built AX "intelligent" typewriters. These machines were similar to many other kinds of typewriters built previously on the line, except they contained computer hardware. Most of the complicated word-processing function add-ons had already been installed by the robot line the day before.

As the typewriters came down the line, we jumped to action. The silence of the early morning factory was broken by the series of buzzes, clicks, and rumblings from steel parts sliding from one place to another on the robot assembly line, and by the deafening whir of electric screwdrivers bolting typewriter parts together. The experienced women performed sets of five small actions every twenty seconds. These consisted, for example, of accurately inserting, positioning, and screwing in typewriter parts, cleaning installed sections, inserting springs, spreading grease over certain areas, or checking typewriter functions. I was amazed at the speed with which these women performed their tasks. Aiko, whom I watched intently, could accurately type out the entire keyboard, test the superscripting, subscripting, and correcting functions as well as fit a plastic cover over the mechanism, all within twenty seconds. She typed as fast as a trained secretary; over five years, the keyboards had become second nature to her.

When I first entered the factory in June 1987, Kojima, one of the factory managers, explained the entire typewriter manufacturing process to me and immediately set me to work installing motors into special holders to be bolted later into the typewriter chassis. I put together about five hundred of these motor-and-holder units, making many mistakes, taking the units apart, and redoing them. Factory work was much more challenging than I had expected. Matsuda and Tomita, the senior workers on the line, taught me how to use the magnetized electric screwdriver properly to pick up screws and set them into place effortlessly.

Matsuda and Tomita had special functions on the line as the designated senior workers. They oversaw the line and were responsible for flawless production. They listened to the workers' complaints and problems and tried to help them. They also taught the factory workers new techniques and made sure that they mastered them. These women have gained much respect during their years in the factory. They came to work in the Nagoya factory after graduating from junior high schools in different cities in Kyushu, one of the southern islands of Japan. They had worked on the line for fifteen years and could fix a typewriter in a matter of minutes. Most women who join the line learn the fundamentals of building typewriters from them and are assigned two or three tasks on the line. Later, the senior workers work them up to the usual five or six tasks depending upon their performance.

The senior workers have seen a great turnover of women on the line. Many workers come to the factory for a year or two before they quit for marriage or other reasons. They are constantly being replaced by fresh crops of young women. The senior workers also oversee the training of young salarymen who work on the factory lines for two weeks as part of their freshman company training, and OLs who are transferred to the factory when the lines are short of laborers. The company justifies these transfers by the policy that employees must all work for the greater good of the company. The workers choose the company, not the job, when they come to Brother. All newly hired employees look to senior workers for assistance. Many of the women identified with Tomita and Matsuda and talked to them about their personal lives as well as about the fundamentals of using a screwdriver.

I was placed on the line on my second day. First, I was given the small jobs of greasing and setting springs into tiny openings of the typewriter chassis. The motions took me about fifteen seconds. Sachiko and Mieko, the women who stood at my sides, completed five motions in seventeen seconds. Sachiko straightened and inserted a typewriter head mechanism into the chassis, screwed another metal part onto the body, and inserted two springs into the back roller. Mieko adjusted the settings of two of the key mechanisms, drilled in the roller, and washed it in strong-smelling cleaning fluid. I was astounded at their speed.

Every day at 9:00, the Chimney Sweep song from "Mary Poppins" played over the loud speaker. It was a signal to the factory women to sit down and rest for exactly sixty seconds. The line paused for a minute. This minute, which passed all too quickly, gave some relief from standing. We could collect our thoughts while we sat on the benches waiting for the buzzer to sound and the line to start up again. Promptly at 9:01, the interrupted flow of typewriters down the line restarted, and it was production as usual.

Some mornings, however, things did not run like clockwork, and we had more time to complete our assembly line tasks. Sometimes there just were not enough parts available to manufacture the daily quota of typewriters, or the robot line did not run as smoothly as expected. Then, Tomita would interrupt the flow of typewriters, screaming down the line, "Hold it!" We finished the typewriter we were working on and did not pass it to the next person until we heard her yell "Next!" and the buzzer sounded again.

At 10:00, a tune from the "Nutcracker Suite" played over the loudspeaker, signaling our ten-minute coffee/bathroom break. We turned off the fluorescent lamps above our workbenches, and the senior workers switched off the main assembly line power. Women marched in droves to the ladies' room or the cafeteria. Some remained at their benches, ate candy, and continued the discussions they had begun early that morning. At 10:08, "Camptown Ladies" played over the loudspeaker, indicating that it was time to return to our workbenches. The line started up again at 10:10, when another loud buzz sounded. We had another one-minute break at 11:00 A.M., after which time dragged until noon. We unanimously agreed that these were the longest fifty-nine minutes in the day. Mieko and Sachiko marked the minutes until noon, yelling encouragement to the women nearby: "Just thirty minutes until lunch time! Only twenty minutes more! Stick it out!" We reminded ourselves that we would be rewarded with a forty-minute sit-down lunch if only we could stick it out until noon.

Finally, "Camptown Ladies" blasted again over the intercom. The lines stopped. We turned off the lamps at our workbenches and walked in groups to the sinks at the sides of the room to scrub with detergent the black grease that had smeared our hands and gloves during work. We draped our gloves, smelling of kerosene, over the wooden benches by the line and walked to the cafeteria.

The factory cafeteria was a large, dingy green room in the southern part of the factory. Workers entered from one end, passed a series of vending machines selling anything from coffee to instant Chinese noodles, and proceeded to the other end of the room to one of the small company-run stores or hot-lunch stalls. The food was not very tasty, but it was inexpensive and filling, and we enjoyed the chance to sit.

Lunchtime at the cafeteria was a social time, as I came to understand it. It was the only time that men and women could actually speak to each other, although few took advantage of this opportunity. Workers stood in long or short lines, depending on which lunch they wanted. The men usually opted for the B-lunch, which consisted of miso soup, a bowl of rice, salad, tofu with ginger and miso flavorings, and fried meat or seafood. Women usually chose to eat small sandwiches from the company store, thick noodles in broth, or the A-lunch, a cold boxed lunch of boiled rice, fried vegetables, and fried meat. There was an unconscious division of the sexes even in the cafeteria lines. And at 350 yen ($2.80), the B-lunch was more expensive and more filling than the A-lunch, which cost 250 yen ($2.00), or the small sandwiches at 80 yen ($.64) each. Most women ate lightly and had ice cream or candies for dessert.

Other options chosen by both sexes were curried rice, boiled eggs, and rice balls with seaweed or fish, sold at the store on the far end of the dining hall. The store also sold ice cream, candy, sandwiches, and pastries during working hours. It was unmanned, and purchases were made on an honor system, with the worker slipping money into a slot in the money box. The older women who ran the food services set out large pots of tea on the long dining hall tables for the rest of the workers.

Factory women carried their trays of food to the long dining hall tables, where the same groups sat together every day. Unlike office workers, factory workers at Brother rarely socialized with the people in their work sections. Some had come to Brother by introduction from friends or relatives and ate with them. Most ate with friends from other work groups.

As at breakfast, women on teams ate together. Three-quarters of the women's softball team worked in the Mizuho factory, and they usually ate in a large group at one long table. Sometimes they invited me and some male engineers to eat with them. These women took enormous pleasure in questioning me relentlessly on the appearance and actions of American men, and in poking fun at the young male engineers, for anything from how they looked that morning to their bachelor status. Once, Hiromi, a young catcher on the team, teased a designer in the sewing machine division: "Yamada-san, you look very handsome today. Do you have a date?" Flattered, he bought ice cream for the team members at his table.

Lunch was the time to relax and to forget about the stresses of work. The men smoked cigarettes. The women made small talk with the men at the tables, but the differences between the sexes were apparent. People sat in their chairs or wandered about outside of the dining hall. Sometimes women from the advertising division would come to the cafeteria to hand out joke computer-dating surveys that humorously matched men and women to unlikely people in the company. Michiyo, a young typewriter inspector, expressed dismay at finding herself paired up with a fifty-year-old married factory administrator in the sewing machine division.

The fun lasted until 12:35 when "Camptown Ladies" played over the loudspeakers once again. In neat formation, the Mizuho workers carried their trays to the bins near the entrance to the cafeteria and put their dishes and chopsticks in tubs of soapy water. Then they walked back to their respective workplaces. At 12:40, bells chimed over the public address system. Tomita-san yelled "It's time" and flipped the power switches to restart the flow of typewriter bodies down the line. We worked until our one-minute sit-down break at 2:00. At 3:00, we got another ten-minute coffee break. One hour before quitting time, Tomita stopped the line, assembling us for a ten-minute general cleanup of the area. The women worked in pairs to carry the trash out to the dumpster, sweep the floors, and wipe down the workbenches with turpentine. These actions promoted general camaraderie and teamwork. Working quickly with a partner meant that you had that much more time to rest until the line started up again. Cleanup was a welcome time since it meant that quitting time was approximately an hour away.

Most days we were allowed to leave the factory at 5:00. Everyone, however, was required to do overtime work when the company was short of workers or needed to produce more than the usual number of machines. We sometimes worked overtime four or five times a week when there was heavy demand, and occasionally we even worked on Saturdays and Sundays. During the early weeks of production of the AX-26 typewriter, the women did overtime about five times a week and worked full nine-hour days on both Saturday and Sunday.

The factory administrators did not force workers to do overtime or to work on weekends, but no one ever voiced a complaint. Factory workers did not consider overtime requests to be unreasonable or unusual. It was understood that they would ungrudgingly work the extra hours if the company needed them, and they did receive compensation for the extra hours they put in. The closest thing to a complaint was when women called the overtime policy "selfish" on the part of the company, but they continued to work with the same fervor and retained the same commitment to their jobs that they had during periods of normal production.

The lives that women led after hours varied. One worker was a mother (Tomoko, chapter five). She had to pick her children up from the sitter's home, clean house, do the shopping, and cook dinner. Overtime work was especially hard on her. Other factory women returned to their dormitories to eat dinner or watch television, knit or talk to friends, do their laundry, and prepare for bed. Others went to night school to get nursery-school teaching certification or high school diplomas so they could eventually leave the line and do work that was less physically demanding and more intellectually challenging (Naomi, chapter five). The women who competed on sports teams were excused from overtime and went straight to the Brother sports grounds or gymnasium after 3:00 to practice for three or four hours before they returned to the dormitory for dinner, bath, and bed.

Factory women went out with their work sections once or twice a month to eat at an inexpensive restaurant or bowl a few games. One day, I went with the women on my line to a self-serve octopus pancake restaurant where we sat around a big table and made octopus pancakes and other dishes. Each serving cost 400 yen ($3.20). In the restaurant, everyone listened intently to Mako's explanation of the best way to make the pancakes and then tried it. Mako, a vivacious girl, dominated the conversation with talk about bowling and her crazy boyfriend, the fisherman. Afterward, we had ice cream and bean jam at the local Sugakiya, a fast-food restaurant serving Chinese noodles, soft ice cream, and other desserts.

On special occasions, the women went in large groups to an inexpensive pub where they could quaff a couple of beers or lemon sours, have dinner, and talk and laugh in loud voices, away from the company of men. At 9:00 P.M., the women who lived in the dormitory left, with ample time to spare for their 9:30 curfew. The other women took the trains back to their homes in various parts of Aichi Prefecture.

Most nights, however, the factory women did not go out. They returned to the dormitory and were the first ones to soak in the bath when the shower and bath room opened at 7:00. Mieko told me that it was very important to "remove my fatigue" with a nice long soak. After the bath, the women sat in their rooms eating sweets and drinking tea with their roommates. They usually watched television—quiz programs, suspense dramas, music programs—whatever was popular at the time. Bedtime came around 11:00 P.M., or much later if the conversation was good or if one became engrossed in a piece of knitting.

I have described a typical day in the life of a factory woman, but not all days are really like this. The lives of the women are unique, and not everyone lives in the dormitory. Women have different roommates or different relationships within the company. The biographies in chapter five bring some of these specifics to light. The differences in work experience are small, however. Women shift bench positions on the line every six weeks, or sometimes when a fellow worker calls in sick, but their work content does not change much. They experience the same breaks every day, see the same coworkers, and listen to the same announcements and music piped in over the public address system.

The content of the work is of little consequence to the factory woman. It does not matter to her whether she drills in a normal head mechanism for a student typewriter or a computerized one for an intelligent word-processing typewriter. The end result for the factory woman is the same. She will use a screwdriver to attach one piece of metal to another, and another tool to adjust the springs.

The few things that affect the factory woman are the seasons and the relationships formed with different members of the workplace. The summers are hot and humid, and the factory becomes infested with microscopic mites that creep into their stockings and bite their legs as they stand on the line. Some women resort to spraying insect poison on their legs to kill the bugs. In the winter the mites disappear. The late spring and autumn bring unceasing rains and gray weather, making the factories appear gloomier and more unpleasant than usual.

Relationships within the workplace have much to do with a factory woman's outlook. Some girls remain cheerful despite the long hours and the monotony. They quickly become favorites in the workplace, lifting everyone's spirits. Factory work is not merely a physical drain but also a mental and spiritual one. It takes only about two weeks for most bodies to get used to the work and the eight hours of standing; but factory women, unlike OLs, find it hard to identify with their work group. They have few opportunities to speak to others in the group, and there is little intellectual stimulation. Frequently the workers actually run out of things to think about.

The work renders the women somewhat helpless. On my line one of the floor supervisors came by, smiled, and patted the women on their bottoms while they worked. When this happened to me, I was infuriated and felt completely powerless. I was working on a typewriter body at the time, and there were machines flowing down the line. The women told me that the supervisor often did that kind of thing, and they could do nothing but ignore it when it happened.

The on-line experiences for men and women are basically the same except for these incidents of harassment. There were only two men, in their late forties, on my line. They packaged and inspected typewriters at the far end. These men, who were not considered by the women to be part of their group, kept to themselves and had little contact with anyone except the senior workers. Despite the similarities in jobs, men receive more benefits than women do. They get monetary compensation when they marry and when they have children. Women do not. Men can be promoted to the position of factory supervisor if they show ambition and work hard enough. Women can become senior workers on the line and gain more responsibilities, but the position of "senior worker" is not official or company-ordained. It comes only with seniority and ambition.

Women usually resort to talking about men and marriage while they work on the line. This, in fact, is their favorite topic. It gets their minds off the work and onto their dreams of a brighter future. For most, marriage and husbands will be their eventual ticket out of the monotony of factory work. Some will stay on the line indefinitely. Many of the women told me that they wanted to marry as soon as possible, to enter into the security of married life. They wanted to end their days at the factory.

CHAPTER THREE

Life in the Sales Office

BEFORE GOING to Japan, I had studied Tom Rohlen's *For Harmony and Strength* for an introduction to social life in a Japanese company. I was fascinated by Rohlen's reports of relationships that formed within the Japanese group, the interactions that ''make hard work meaningful'' or pose as a ''cancer in the organization and the source of great individual unhappiness'' (1974, 93). He describes the male experience in the Japanese bank Uedagin and suggests that the lifetime employment system of Japanese companies fosters strong ties, while high turnover does the opposite in ''diluting human relationships, emphasizing the impersonal, sharpening differences in background and interest.''

Office ladies at Brother leave the company after several years of service. Are the relationships for females within the work group diluted? I pondered the roles of the OLs in the office work group. How do these women perceive group obligations? How do OLs who serve tea and do trivial assignments view their work and their work group? Entering a work section in the sales office allowed me to examine these perceptions first hand.

My introduction to a Japanese office came on June 10, 1986, when I arrived at Nagoya International Airport. Two OLs, Ms. Suzuki and Ms. Matsumura, and a salaryman, Mr. Hayashi, came to meet me. I recognized them by the blue company logo bags that they were carrying. They waited patiently as I went through customs and told the customs officer that I had no contraband or gifts of high value. Then, they greeted me with the standard ''Nice to meet you'' and carried my bags to the car.

In the car, Hayashi and Matsumura introduced themselves as employees from the personnel division, and Suzuki as an employee from the sales office. I had already been told of Suzuki in a letter from the personnel division that read, ''Miss Suzuki will take care of you while you are in Nagoya. Please contact her directly if you have any questions or problems.'' My initial reaction to the letter was surprise that the company would actually give a new employee what amounted to ''guardian'' status. At twenty-one and in my third year of college, I did not need someone to take me on trips, to oversee my study of Japanese, and to be with me constantly, but the company apparently felt otherwise. It was understood that female foreigners, like young women in Nagoya, lack direction and experience in Japanese adult society and might be led astray. We must be watched carefully. Americans, it was thought, lacked the proper knowledge to get about in Japanese society and needed special tutoring.

As my ''governess,'' Suzuki taught me the basics of office life. She also sacrificed much of her personal time for our ''professional'' relationship. She accompanied me on all business trips, and whenever I went out for dinner or drinks with anyone related to our work section. Suzuki rarely left my side while I worked in the planning office. She masterfully fulfilled her obligation to the director of the sales office, who had assigned her this job. Of course, she still had her other work as an OL, which she had to finish too. I was surprised at the number of ''after-six'' hours she spent doing things with me, just because our boss had asked her to.

There is definitely a perceived sense of obligation that comes with membership in a Japanese work group. The welcoming committee sacrificed hours of their personal time, unpaid, to pick me up at the airport. Hayashi paid for our dinners out of his own pocket and drove me to the Brother dormitory in his car. White-collar workers identify strongly with the company, and many times this compels them to do work outside of their official responsibilities. Other forms of after-six work entail such time-consuming duties as chaperoning the handball team's hiking trips, arranging trips for the work section, choosing wedding presents for the boss, and volunteering to be a company representative at a weekend import fair. I came to understand work group voluntarism to be the norm rather than the exception.

I gained a deeper understanding of the obligation felt by office employees when I joined the work group. A formal initiation took place the following day. The director asked Suzuki to give me a tour of the Kamimaezu office building to familiarize me with the sights and sounds of Brother Sales. She began with the first-floor showroom. All of the office machines sat on the shelves, ready for demonstration to prospective customers by beautiful young OLs who had diligently studied the appropriate instruction manuals and were able to deliver memorized speeches on the virtues of each machine.

On the third floor of the Kamimaezu office building, most of the official business takes place. Suzuki showed me the various meeting rooms where the male executives sat about, chain-smoked their omnipresent "Mild Seven" cigarettes, and discussed the company's future. In the large kitchen were various coffee machines. OLs worked in those kitchens preparing tea and other refreshments for the men who attended the meetings. There were no female executives.

The rest of the floors housed the different work sections. The design of each floor was simple: a large room where everyone worked, two washrooms, a kitchen, and a small lobby between the elevator and the entrance to the large room. The desks, organized by job assignments, were arranged in long, compact rows. Salarymen and OLs working on similar projects were clustered in different places in the room. A couple of mornings during the year, the bosses posted seat changes. Everyone in the section moved their desks accordingly. The management—the section chiefs, division chiefs, and director—sat apart from the rest of the group, near the windows. This gave them an excellent vantage point to oversee the work of their employees.

Suzuki and the director of Brother Sales accompanied me to every floor as I was formally initiated into the group. The director introduced me to the management on each floor and explained the purpose of each section. Then he made a short speech: "Let's welcome Jeannie Lo to Brother Sales. She is now a member of the seventh floor, so please feel free to ask her anything and to teach her many things." Different people in the office stood up, bowed, and greeted me. In name, I had joined the group and could be called on to carry out the requests of my superiors—boss, salarymen, and senior OLs. I was given calling cards of my own with the Brother logo. Acceptance into the group meant that I would serve tea and defer to the men in the workplace.

My education proceeded slowly. On the first day, I learned the small points of calling card etiquette. I learned that it was impolite to put someone else's calling card in one's back pocket. You must keep the other person's card on display on the table in front of you until he puts your card away, or until an appropriate period of time has passed. Doing otherwise is considered rude. I talked to different OLs in my work section, who were so polite that it made me feel awkward. They offered me cookies and tea, and they continued to serve me coffee and tea every day for several weeks. Members of my work group had conflicting feelings of closeness and alienation toward me: proximity because we were Asian, and distance because I was American. This alienation translated to extreme politeness on their part. They wanted to be close, but in being so polite to me, they did not treat me like the others and kept me out of their group. There were many barriers to understanding. At first, I felt no obligation to the workplace, and they did not expect that I—an American—would. It took a couple of months before I found a comfortable niche in the work group and could walk through the hallways unnoticed by others, or be invited to participate in people's lives outside the company.

An after-six conversation with Tadashi, a young salaryman, confirmed my sense of dichotomy. We had become good friends in the research and development section by the time I asked him, "What do people in the company really think of me, a Chinese-American?" He pulled me aside and confided: "It's really strange to look at you and to think that you are American. You look Japanese. You're not Chinese either. You were raised in the United States."

After a while, the OLs began to confide in me too. Perhaps this was *because* I was an outsider, and some things are easier to say to someone who is not ingrained in Japanese ways. There would be no negative repercussions. I made slow progress in gaining acceptance. During the first month, they invited me to go shopping with them. After two months, I went to bars and discos with them and spent weekends at their homes. I worked hard to dissolve the obvious differences between us, but the rifts in understanding were wide. The women were surprised that I could eat Japanese food (and actually liked it), that I could sit in the Japanese style, kneeling with my feet and calves folded underneath my thighs, and, most of all, that I could make myself understood in Japanese. Sometimes it was difficult for them to feel comfortable with me, a woman from Harvard. To them, Harvard was like Tokyo University, a source of great minds and company presidents. The OLs were sensitive to such notions of hierarchy and admired these institutions and the people associated with them.

I made many observations during my six months as an office lady. I came to the office deeply aware of how different I was from the Japanese OL. Not only had I not grown up in Japan, but I had joined the company under special circumstances. I entered the work group in June, not April, when other OLs are usually initiated. For all these reasons, I had to seek special ways to gain acceptance. I did my best to mimic the OLs. I spent mornings in the office talking about clothes, fashion, and men. I participated in lunchtime conversations and insisted that I do things alone, without Suzuki's help. I believed, for reasons of self-esteem and research, that I should be an OL in my own right, not just a charge of an appointed "guardian."

Acceptance, I found, is closely tied to one's sense of obligation. I discovered as an OL that I had to be somewhat subservient. There is a strict hierarchy in the office, with the management at the top and the salarymen and OLs below. To be accepted into the work group, one must demonstrate knowledge of one's position within that hierarchy, one's obligations to everyone else, and one's dedication to preserving the special relationships. OLs and salarymen rarely question the decisions of management. The management is obligated to "take care" of inferiors. For example, the director and division chiefs treat members of their sections to dinner in local restaurants or their homes at least once a month.

I examined OLs' own views of their position in the hierarchy by observing over one hundred days of life in the office. Superficially, each day was much the same. The workday started officially at 9:00 A.M. The domestic duties of the "on-duty OL" began at 8:30 A.M. The women normally took turns preparing the office for the arrival of the other members of the group. The on-duty OL boiled water for morning tea service and tidied up the kitchen. She turned on the copy machines, the lights in the bathroom, and the air-conditioning unit so the office would be ready for work at 9:00 when the others arrived. She also wiped all of the telephones and desktops clean with a damp rag. Many times, she lifted the piles of paper and personal belongings to clean the vinyl covering the desks. She served tea when most of the employees arrived, and then later when the bosses came in, minutes before 10:00.

The rest of the OLs reached the office by 8:55 A.M. Everyone seemed to arrive at the same time, filling up the elevators of the Kamimaezu building. OLs and salarymen bowed "Good morning" to each other and entered the elevators, the men allowing the ladies to go first. People exchanged small talk on the way up. Men left the elevator silently at their floors. Women said "Excuse me" as they left and then pressed the "close door" button, making the elevator doors shut soon after they stepped out. The salarymen stopped for a quick smoke in the small lobby on their floor; smoking in the office was frowned upon. OLs went to their lockers at the far end of the room, where they put their handbags away and touched up their makeup. Everyone was assigned a locker with his or her name on it. The men, however, chose not to use the lockers and hung their jackets on hangers near the front entrance. Some women looked out the window into the neighboring office building where the salarymen and OLs did mandatory calisthenics led by the section chiefs. Iwata, the section chief of my division, smiled happily and swung his arms, remarking, "We wouldn't even think of doing that kind of thing here!"

Salarymen and OLs went to the magnetic bulletin board to move their nameplates to the proper heading: "present," "out of the building," or "business trip." "Out of the building" indicated that the employee was conducting business within Nagoya, and "business trip" meant that he or she was out of the city. There was another column on the bulletin board where people wrote notes on exactly where they were and when they would return. Such organization was necessary for the bosses to keep track of the workers, and especially for the OLs who answered the phones. They were able to inform clients of the schedules of different people in the office at a glance.

Promptness was the key to the office. There were no timecards to punch in. No one kept notes on who arrived early or late. There was a tacit understanding that one would always be on time unless there were extenuating circumstances. Members of a workplace did not comment directly on a coworker's tardiness but talked about it among themselves. The late worker lost face and was treated with disapproval. To maintain good relations with coworkers, one had to be prompt or have a very good excuse for tardiness. The only

people not affected by these social pressures were the top management—the director and division chiefs. All others were at their
desks by 9:00 when work officially started.

The on-duty OL came around with a tray of hot tea for the men.
The other OLs served themselves tea or coffee. Men sat at their
desks reading company reports or economic newspapers. Some OLs
used the photocopiers while others punched documents into word
processors. The rest sat at their desks discussing the dates they had
had the night before or things that had happened at home. Conversation was lighthearted. A typical conversation that I recorded went
as follows:

"Hiroshi and I went to the Italian Tomato [a popular restaurant].
I had a good time. He wants to take me out again on Wednesday."

"Eh? That's great. All I did was go shopping. The sales aren't
very good this time of the year, but I got some nice accessories,
like these earrings."

"They're chic! I saw them in a magazine."

The conversations went on while the bosses were out of the room
in meetings. Mornings were slow times at the office. Sometimes
the bosses gave women difficult assignments, but most of the time
their work only took up two or three hours of the day. The bosses
had managed Brother workers for decades and had not changed
their views of worker roles. Men did the challenging work; OLs
served tea, did light clerical work, and, as "office flowers,"
brightened up the office with their presence. OLs tried to appear as
the stereotypical *ojosama*, proper and sophisticated young ladies.
They consulted the fashion magazines to assemble *ojosama* outfits
for the office. Many were concerned with appearances. If they were
even slightly overweight, they could expect a comment from the
bosses.

Around men, many OLs were *burikko*. (*Buri* comes from *furi*, or
pretense, and *ko* means child. A *burikko* is a grown woman who
acts like a child. She may be sexually active, but she feigns
innocence.) The men enjoyed this pretense. One commented, "*Bu-*

rikko are cute. It's nice to have them around.'' Consistent with the *burikko* act, women cluttered their desks with toys and pins of Disney characters. By pretending to be children, OLs attempted to attract the attention of men who might take care of them; they did not act like women who were ready to take on serious responsibilities.

The director usually arrived a little before 10:00 looking slightly ragged, giving the appearance that he had worked late at the office the night before, or that he had just returned from a business trip. The director of Brother Sales kept an electric razor in the locker by his desk. He walked briskly to his desk, sat down, shaved, and made phone calls. Yoko, his secretary, rushed up to his desk with a hot cup of coffee, or a refreshingly chilled glass of barley tea in the summer. He sipped his coffee or tea as he shaved.

Some mornings, I heard him scream ''Jeannie-chan'' (chan is a filial term for an inferior). I learned to run up to his desk like the other women, with pen and paper in hand to write down his many orders or to take notes on different things that he would tell me. With a quick wave of his hand, he would send me away and call the next person. At first, I could not help but feel insulted by this treatment, even though the other OLs were treated in the same manner. I wondered if the OLs around me felt the same tinge of resentment that I did when the director waved me away with a slight gesture of his hand. They said they didn't, but I knew that criticizing superiors is taboo. I wondered if it was something that an OL could get used to. I was never comfortable with it, but I decided to keep my opinions to myself.

The director left for meetings on the third floor or in another part of the city shortly after 10:00. Yoko moved the small magnetic button on the board to ''out of the building'' or ''business trip'' and made the appropriate notes in the column next to his name.

At 10:00 A.M., most of the workers took a break for coffee. The breaks were not designated ones, and there were no bells over the public address system announcing them. The management left it to us to take breaks, and to the men to go for a quick smoke in the lobby. Smoking by women was frowned upon. OLs kept jars of candy on their desks, amid their Mickey Mouse paraphernalia and the Hello Kitty insignia items. Iwata sent an OL to the local supermarket to buy candy when the jars began to empty. Some OLs distributed souvenir snacks from a trip or cookies and small cakes given out as gifts from an affiliated company. It was workplace etiquette to buy confections for one's colleagues on at least every third business trip. The gifts usually consisted of pastries, crackers, specialty teas, fruit, or chocolates, which were distributed among the workers. Anything left over was served at meetings on the third floor.

By 10:15, men lowered their faces into books of financial figures, and OLs went off to photocopy. A steady stream of messengers, mailmen, and clients went through the office. Work proceeded rather slowly until noon. OLs busied themselves with telephone calls and typing spreadsheets of information for the men. The workers watched the clock until noon, when they dropped what they were doing to rise from their seats and move to the elevators. Men ate at the local lunch shops and coffee shops in Ohsu, the neighborhood around the Kamimaezu building filled with family-run restaurants and mom-and-pop stores selling traditional arts and crafts. At coffee shops customers could get a set lunch of miso soup, cabbage salad with mayonnaise, fried meat, or fish and rice. Other popular lunchtime meals were spaghetti or curried rice.

Women bought riceballs or bread in the Ohsu shops. The bread, stuffed with sweet bean jams, egg salad, or chicken curry, was filling. The OLs usually bought two large pieces of bread or three riceballs filled with fish or seaweed. Four rice balls was considered excessive, and two suggested that the OL was on a diet. "So you're only having two riceballs. Is that enough? Are you on a diet?" Women also had yogurt drinks or salads with their meals. Diets and men were popular topics of conversation. It was not unusual for one OL to tell another, "You've really gained weight, haven't you?'' There was definitely an emphasis on appearance, perhaps linked to the desire to attract a husband.

After buying lunch, the OLs returned to the office. They rarely ate out, because that was expensive. Buying bread or riceballs usually cost less than 300 yen ($2.50); eating out would cost anywhere from 500 yen for the cheapest bowl of noodles to about 1,000 yen for a fancy set lunch. The OLs who brought boxed lunches from home did not go out at noon to buy food but stayed in to make tea for the rest of us. We usually gathered around one of the meeting tables and ate lunch. With no men in the office, the women acted differently. They talked in loud voices about the news or fashion or made fun of the men. They rarely talked about their bosses, and when they did, they praised them. They were afraid of offending the others and placing stresses on workplace relationships. Some of the women dropped their *burikko* pretenses, but others did not. Talking about the cicadas one summer, for example, one OL— speaking like the stereotypical *burikko*—said, ''Those cicadas are coming back this summer. Euuh, I hate them. Yeucch!'' Another woman retorted, ''They're not as bad as cockroaches! They don't have as many germs.'' Another answered, ''I think they do. They have horrible eyes and they make that terrible sound, 'Mi, mi, mi, mi.' They're just terrible.'' I mentioned that 1987 was a big year for cicadas and received a round of ''That's disgusting'' in reply. Other times, they talked about Yoshino, the head salaryman in the office. They commented, ''He even walks funny,'' or ''He's already in his thirties and he's still single. It's really unbelievable.'' Such talk would go on until 12:35, when the women started to pick up their lunch bags and clear the emptied cups of tea onto a tray. One woman washed the cups; the others cleaned the table with a rag. Many OLs brushed their teeth in the bathroom. Few salarymen did, as they were usually rushing back to their desks to make phone calls and do business. Everyone returned to their seats before 12:40.

The directors and division chiefs who were in the office that day returned shortly after lunch. The directors read newspapers or went to meetings in the afternoon. People continued to work on their projects throughout the day. Women typed, answered the phones, or went to the stationery store across the street to buy office supplies. There was a cabinet for ballpoint pens, automatic pencils, rulers, Post-it note pads, erasers, staplers, legal pads, and Brother letterhead stationery, and when the supply of a certain item ran low, an OL went to the store to replenish it. They kept notes on office expenditures, from the flow of petty cash to the dispensing of bullet train tickets used for business travel. This bookkeeping duty is similar to Japanese housewives' responsibility of accounting for family expenses.

Every OL had a different assignment in the office, the complexity and interest of which corresponded to the woman's seniority and educational level. This was true for almost every workplace, in either Brother Sales or Brother Industries. The director of sales assigned Suzuki and Kawasaki the most difficult OL jobs. Suzuki, in her third year at the company, was a graduate of the prestigious Ochanomizu Women's College in Tokyo. Kawasaki had graduated from a lesser-known college in Tokyo and started off with clerical duties of a level higher than those performed by graduates of junior colleges. Suzuki translated English text into Japanese, did accounting work, and became my guardian. The last duty was probably the most demanding, since my Japanese was not very good and her spoken English was nonexistent. Kawasaki was placed in charge of designing and producing ''Hows,'' a newsletter for the buyers of Brother word processors. She used her artistic talent and creativity in this project to produce something that became a big hit with the buyers.

Other OLs were less fortunate. One girl who graduated from a junior college in Nagoya photocopied newspaper and magazine articles on office machine technology and business and distributed copies to each of the section chiefs in Brother Sales. Kazuko, with only a high school education, spent her days drawing graphs for the salarymen in her division. She found her job less than challenging.

She idled away her time, talking to other OLs at the desks around her. Kazuko did not take her job seriously, and the others in the workplace excused her. A twenty-five-year-old commented, "Kazuko is only eighteen years old. She's barely an adult."

The most extreme case of on-the-job boredom was one young woman who called me because she wished to tell me about her situation yet remain anonymous. She said: "I called you because I want you to know. I am an OL in one of the industrial sections. I'm afraid that you may miss me when you conduct your research. I wonder if you have this in America. I sit in a chair from 9:00 A.M. to 6:00 P.M. My only job is to answer telephones. I sit in front of my division chief so I can't read or pass my time doing other things. It's horrible. There are hours of the day when nothing happens at all." OLs in the research and development division assured me that this woman's story was true. They shook their heads and said, "It's a pity." We silently mourned the deplorable waste of a fellow OL's potential.

The second break came at 3:00 P.M. The OLs distributed snacks and served tea to men. Once every couple of weeks, Section Chief Ii sent Masumi to Winchell's Donuts down the street to buy a basketful of "munchkins" for the OLs and the salarymen. Ii's family was closely linked to the wealth and power of the company. His father started the Brother Real Estate Company and amassed great wealth through the buying and selling of choice property. Unlike other section chiefs, he found extreme pleasure in keeping our candy jars filled with doll-shaped sweets, and in taking his workers out to lunch and dinner. Ii was wealthy to the degree that these expenditures were of little consequence to him.

OLs worked intently from 3:10 until 6:00 P.M., when all of their assignments had to be finished. Women who completed their work early exchanged small talk and waited until closing time. Some ate candy and talked about the sales in Sakae, Nagoya's shopping district, or about other members of the work group. Again, they rarely mentioned their work. Few found their assigned clerical tasks to be thought-provoking or worthy of mention.

The workday ended officially at 6:00, but rarely did salarymen leave at that time. They worked overtime almost every night to convince the management that they were good candidates for promotion. It looked bad for a salaryman to leave before the others in the workplace, and if they worked late they were said to be truly serious about their work. Yet no one ever talked about a "serious" office lady. OLs were supposed to leave the office a couple of minutes after 6:00 to go shopping or return home. The management in my section never gave us work that could not be accomplished at a leisurely pace during an eight-hour day.

I asked women in the research and development division what OLs thought about their jobs. "What does an OL think when she serves tea to the men in the office? When she is assigned to sit by the telephone for hours doing work that is shamefully dull?"

One woman, Matsui, answered definitively, "The relationships in the office are a matter of *shigarami*." My first thought was that the *shi* of *shigarami* referred to work, as in *shigoto* (work), and that *garami* was a derivative of *karamiau* (involve or entangle). This interpretation was wrong, but I was not far off the mark when I envisioned entanglements. Matsui drew the following figure into my notebook:

"This," she said, "is *shigarami*, a weir, a fence of brush that is used to trap fish in a river." She justified her statement: "*Shigarami* is a word commonly used by the Japanese to describe themselves. I've even heard the man at the local fishmarket use it. It refers to the delicate way in which human relationships hold together. If one bond breaks, then the whole structure falls apart. People are careful not to harm these relationships." *Shigarami*

applies not only to work and the office but also to every aspect of life in Japan. It is a metaphor for the underlying structure of Japanese relationships.

Matsui explained how *shigarami* fits into the lives of the OLs. It describes a basic structure where people are afraid of jeopardizing special human relationships for fear that they will be excluded, or that they will not serve the good of the whole. The structure is one that makes demands and ties individuals to certain actions. In other contexts, *shigarami* is used to denote a binding structure. It is used to describe the "fetters of love" and the "compelling force of human compassion." Similarly, OLs are bound by their roles. Matsui explained that "An OL may not enjoy serving tea, but she does so out of obligation to her work group. Refusing to serve tea places her relationships with her bosses and peers in jeopardy. Her bosses will not regard her as a dedicated worker. Her fellow OLs may think that she is putting on airs, by refusing to do something that they must do every day. An OL acquiesces because she doesn't want to ruin the relationship."

Shigarami is used, Matsui explained, in a way similar to *amae,* a theory of indulgence that Takeo Doi explained in *The Anatomy of Dependence*. She continued: "If a superior doesn't want to do a project and gives it to his subordinate, the subordinate will do the work out of perceived friendship or dependence on the superior. That is *amae*. We have a *shigarami* structure when the superior gives his subordinate an order. The subordinate has no special emotional attachment to the boss, but carries out the order so he won't damage the existing work relationships."

It appears that everyone understands their position in society. By carrying out certain roles, men and women maintain harmony in their relationships. They work selflessly for the greater good of the whole. Chie Nakane draws similarities between Japanese society and the household. In the case of OLs, many leave their home to live in the company dormitories; their lives focus on the company, and the company becomes the home. There is an obligation to work for the greater good of the household, and it is dangerous to tamper with human relationships and expectations. The idea that women identify with their company—as they did with their household—is seen in the domesticity of the women in the office and in office attitudes. Nakane adds that "in Japan, it has always been believed that individual morality and mental attitudes have an important bearing on mental and productive power. Loyalty toward the company has been highly regarded" (1970, 16). Nakane suggests that the Japanese belong to a "frame," a group or company, and derive a sense of security from this relationship. Without a frame, a person is not considered to be normal. An OL must defer and act according to the rules of the frame (the company work group). By observing these rules and accepting her designated role in the workplace, she maintains the *shigarami* structure and her good standing in the office group. Those who do not agree with the status quo of the work group must adjust their behavior or leave.

CHAPTER FOUR

"Happy Dormitory Life"

THE GRAND SHRINE of Ise in Mie Prefecture is famous for its fortifications. The many gates and fences stand to protect the sanctity of the inner parts from the defiling influences of the outside world. Purity is sealed in. Corruption is held out. In a similar way, the eight-story Aoi ryo—Hollyhock dormitory—protects its young unmarried residents from perceived corruption by the outside. Aoi dormitory has another social function as well: Brother not only protects its women but molds them into fine marriage prospects and nudges them onto the next step. It expects its female employees to marry and leave the company, making room for young replacements.

When the young women leave their homes to work, paternal control is transferred from the family to the company. The Aoi dormitory management assumes the role of the parent, and in doing so, it feels justified in treating the women as young, unmarried daughters. Personnel division employees agree that most of the rules have been written with fifteen-year-old junior high school students in mind, and that they should not apply to the twenty-eight year-olds in the dormitory. They add, however, "With the dormitory structure that we have, the parents of the girls need not worry. They are well taken care of. There is no way that they can get into trouble."

Fences are just one means of protecting the chastity of the women. To reach the lobby of the concrete dormitory, one must penetrate several barriers. The first obstacle is a green cast-iron fence with spikes and barbed wire running along the top. There are only three points of entry through this fence. Two sections of the gate slide back and forth to permit the entry of cars, delivery trucks, bicycles, and women. One of these sliding doors is at the front of the dormitory, and most people enter and leave through this gate. The sliding gate in the back of the dormitory is for cyclists. Women on sports teams bicycle to work and to practices. They return to the dormitory through the back gates, store their bikes behind the building, and walk to the main entrance. They pass the reception area before they change their shoes and go upstairs to their rooms.

The third opening of the first barrier is a small cast-iron door next to the front sliding gate. The door is normally locked from the inside. The front and the back sliding gates are open from 6:00 A.M. until 9:30 P.M. every day. Anyone who breaks the 9:30 curfew or leaves the dorm earlier than 6:00 with the required special permission of the personnel division must pass through the cast-iron door. All "after-hours" passage in and out of Aoi dormitory is conducted through this door. The dormitory supervisor keeps the key and controls all such traffic through the gate.

Passing through the front sliding gate is easy enough during normal hours. One enters through the open gate into a small concrete courtyard. The dormitory supervisor has planted shrubs on the sides for aesthetic appeal. The company has also planted tall bushes along the inside of the first gate. Bushes serve not only to soften the appearance of the gate but also to block any attempt to look into the dormitory rooms. Walking past the plants and the courtyard, one passes through two glass doors before reaching the reception area. These glass doors lock from the inside and are only open from 6:00 A.M. to 9:30 P.M.

Stationed at an office in the reception area are the supervisor, his wife (whom all of the residents call *ryobosan*, or dormitory mother), and two "older sisters," young dormitory residents who have been hired to assist the dormitory management. They greet all of the dormitory residents and visitors. The dormitory supervisor is an elderly salaryman from the personnel division, chosen for his paternal nature. The selection committee usually decides upon a married man with grown children. The man they choose gives up his life in the office to manage the dormitory. It is common practice for the Brother management to change their employees' work sections without much advance notice. Once assigned the position of dormitory supervisor, the salaryman and his wife move into the dorm's first-floor apartment.

It is the responsibility of the wife to help her husband manage the dormitory and enforce the rules and regulations. The couple will go uncomplainingly to their new life, for the work content of an employee is beyond his or her control. The management frequently acts upon its prerogative to change the type of work an employee does, for the greater good of the company. Young salarymen are sent to foreign countries for internships as long as five years with only two weeks' notice. Likewise, the elderly couple willingly moves into their new home in Aoi dormitory.

Moving is a change not merely of residence but of lifestyle. For their seven-year tenure, the couple will act as guardians of the young women in the dormitory. I realized the full extent of their involvement while observing the farewell ceremonies for the previous supervisor and his wife in 1986. An administrator from the personnel division stood on the stage in the dining room, where all of the residents had gathered, and announced: "As you may all know, Haneda is leaving the dormitory soon, as his seven-year term is over. We will notify you as soon as we select a new dormitory supervisor." Haneda stood up and spoke to the young women. His speech, though short and simple, brought tears to everyone's eyes. He said, "I'm very sad to leave you all. I tried to do my best for you. I will always think of you as if you were my true daughters." Noriko, one of the dormitory older sisters in 1986, gave the

Hanedas a farewell gift from the women in the dormitory and thanked them for taking good care of the residents, for talking to them about their problems, and for coming to them when they were sick in bed. Everyone then returned to their rooms, tearful and silent.

The older sisters, unlike the supervisor and his wife, do not have a set term in the dormitory; they stay until they leave the company. The personnel division chooses young high school graduates who seem congenial and ready to devote themselves to the lives of their ''younger sisters.'' Aiko, twenty-four, and Noriko, twenty-five, were the older sisters in 1986 and 1987. They both started as older sisters when they were eighteen, after graduating from high school in nearby prefectures. Their lives were quite different from those of OLs or factory women. They did most of their work in the little office by the reception area. Their jobs got them up before 6:00 A.M. and kept them busy until 11:00 P.M., seven days a week. They had no time clocks to punch and could sometimes take the afternoon off, but they frequently worked longer hours than other women in the company; they were older sisters twenty-four hours a day.

Noriko and Aiko took turns waking up before the rest of the dormitory residents to open the main kitchen, the activity rooms, and the dining hall for the cleaners. By 6:00 A.M., all of these duties had been completed and they sat in the reception area until 9:00 A.M., greeting each dormitory resident as she left for work.

Their administrative duties began when all of the young women in the dormitory had gone to work. Some days they were very busy. They made posters for the lobby announcing special company events, a handball game, an import fair, and signups for trips to the mountains, beer gardens, and parties with the young bachelors of the company men's dormitories. Different posters decorated the walls of the lobby each week. The older sisters kept dormitory records of cleaning assignments and meals, inspected cleaned rooms, contacted dry cleaners, food services, and handymen, and answered phone calls. After completing these duties, they knitted, watched television, or chatted. Sometimes Aiko would read magazines and wait for phone calls while Noriko went shopping in the department stores of Sakae.

After 5:00, the factory workers returned to Aoi and were greeted by the older sisters. The volume of phone calls increased. At 6:00, Noriko would watch the office while Aiko went to volleyball practice. She made sure that the bath was ready for the residents at 7:30, and that the dining hall was open for dinner.

As part of the office staff, these women kept notes on who entered and who left the dormitory. Only the dorm residents, cleaning ladies and cooks, the elderly woman who ran the small dormitory snack shop, handymen, and company employees with special permission were allowed passage. Guests (both family and friends) had to be met by the reception window, under the watchful eyes of the supervisor and the older sisters. Even the so-called lobby was off-limits to visitors.

Both older sisters knew who was in the dormitory and who had left to go shopping or on a date. Most residents made small talk with them before they left the dormitory. Aiko and Noriko were attentive to what we had to tell them; hence, the office was a center of information on the residents. Especially during the first years of their tenure, the supervisor and his wife often consulted the older sisters about the women and the management of the dormitory. Most of the residents were fond of the two older sisters. Aiko tried to mother the rest of the women, telling them to eat properly and to take care of their health. She was given the nickname "Mother" for what we deemed to be an unnecessary concern for our well-being. She often visited our rooms for light conversation before she went to bed.

After bidding "I'm home" to the congregation at the reception area, each dormitory resident turns her nameplate over to expose its red face. Every resident has to fill out the proper forms and get permission for overnight leaves. The supervisor records the absences—and the reasons for them—on the tag board.

As soon as the women put on their slippers at the foyer and walked into the lobby, they have successfully passed through all of the physical barriers from the outside. They are home, in the security of Aoi dormitory. Through the side exit of the foyer, women enter the lobby, a large room with wall-to-wall carpeting, three brown sofas, a color television set with a sign on it saying "Until 22:00" (10:00 P.M.), and a newspaper rack. Women usually sit there after their baths in the evening or before work in the morning, reading newspapers and chatting. There is often a large group sitting in front of the television set watching popular shows like "Best Ten" (featuring Japan's teenage idols), cartoons, "suspense drama," or romantic situation comedies.

The lobby is the heart of the dormitory, the center of all activities. From automatic vending machines in the far-left corner of the room women can buy soda, yogurt drinks, and milk. Its many exits connect directly to the dining hall, the bathroom and first-floor toilets, the reception area, the hall where sewing, knitting, tea ceremony, and flower arrangement are taught, a special reception room for the guests of the supervisor, his private apartment, and the stairs and elevators leading up to the seven other floors. The dorm supervisor rarely invites guests to his home or to these reception rooms, for the protection of the women.

Each rooming group keeps their room key on hooks in the lobby. None of these room keys is ever taken from the dormitory, and all of the suitemates share one key. The last person to leave the suite takes the key off the hook, opens the door of the room, and hangs the key on another hook in a glass case outside the dormitory office. Independent ownership of keys is discouraged. The system encourages the women to be dependent on each other; in small, cohesive groups, they are less likely to get in trouble, and they tend to talk more about men and marriage.

With keys in hand, the women go to their rooms. Usually four women share two small four-and-a-half tatami mat rooms. Every suite in Aoi ryo is identical, numbered according to floor and room. The supervisor puts plastic nameplates in the holders on the sides of the doors. Opening the flimsy wooden door, one steps into a small area with a tiled floor, a sink, and overhead racks for storing dishes and towels. There are also small shelves and a mirror above the sink. Below the sink are buckets, a broom, and a couple of dust rags. Everyone leaves their dormitory slippers on the tiled floor before they step up into the small common room.

The four girls in each suite share the four large closets, four sets of drawers, a coffee table, and a tiny dresser in the living room. In winter the coffee table is traded in for a short table with an internal heating unit; the women keep warm by sitting with their legs stretched under this table. Thus, the central small table becomes an established place for conversation where, after bathing, women sit and talk about men. Most women wanted boyfriends and fiancés; some of them had them. I was invited—as a third person—on several "dates" by friends in the dormitory who wanted to show their boyfriends off, and I came to understand that having a boyfriend was a real achievement.

Every suite has a balcony. By pulling away the orange drapes and the filthy sliding screen that collects dust and dirt from nearby factories, the women can leave the living room and step out onto the balcony. Many women set up clotheslines to dry laundry. The dormitory management encourages domesticity in women, unlike the men, who have automatic washers and dryers that they can use any time. They also have a regular janitorial staff that scrubs the bath, the changing rooms, and the bathrooms and tidies up the dining halls and hallways. The women do all of these chores themselves. In effect, we were being trained to be good cleaners, so that we could be good housewives one day.

Another set of orange drapes divides the living room and bedroom, where two sets of bunkbeds are separated by a walkway so narrow that only one person at a time can fit. The wooden bunkbed frames are built into the structure of the room, and short wooden ladders lead to the top bunks. A small pull-out desk, shelves, and a fluorescent lamp at the head of the bed complete the furnishings. Long curtains can be pulled across the length of the bed for privacy.

In 1986, about one hundred women lived in this 125-suite dormitory with a capacity of eight hundred. Approximately seventy remained in 1987. The appreciated yen and intensified trade friction lowered company profits in 1986, so it could only afford to hire a few OLs and a total of fifty salarymen and engineers. No freshmen OLs or factory women came in 1987 to replenish the ranks of the women leaving Aoi dormitory for the usual reasons of marriage, new jobs, or "old age" (women were not allowed to live in the dorm after they turned twenty-nine). Despite the 50 percent vacancy rate, seventy women remained crowded in groups of three and four in 1987.

Aoi dormitory management encourages turnover by making the dormitory conditions somewhat uncomfortable. Many of the women do not enjoy being crowded into small rooms and look to the first marriage proposal that they receive as a way out. Hitomi, an office lady who lived at Aoi dormitory, confided, "X from Toyota asked me to marry him. I really don't know what to do. I hardly know him, and during the short time that we've dated [three months], we've fought a lot. I don't love him but I'm getting old, and I may never have another chance to marry. I want to leave this dormitory. They're too strict." Three months later, the twenty-four-year-old Hitomi left the dormitory. Within six months she was a housewife in Tokyo.

Other women find other ways out. Kuniko commented, "I don't want to be crowded. I'm tired of living in this dormitory. There are too many rules. I don't want to share a suite with the other girls anymore." She moved from the dorm to her own apartment in Nagoya. Living alone was a big step for Kuniko. Many people in Nagoya held fast to their moral convictions that "nice girls" just didn't have their own apartments. Kuniko was not sexually promiscuous; she was just tired of sharing a suite with three other women and left, risking social branding as a woman with loose morals. Some did not share her views. They could not understand why anyone would want to live alone. One girl said, "I'm really happy to live with other people. I think that it would be scary and lonely to be all by yourself in the suite." Since I lived alone, these women often called on me and tried to get me to knit and join in other group activities. They believed that I suffered from loneliness and could not understand why I actually enjoyed living by myself. I slowly came to appreciate the comfort that they felt in their groups. They depended on each other and substituted this for the close family ties that they had left behind at home.

To encourage mutual understanding, the management of Aoi dormitory for the most part tries to match up women with similar work or extracurricular interests. A floor-by-floor analysis of the dormitory reveals an internal hierarchy. The prized handball team—the stars of the company because they won the 1986 Aichi Prefecture championship—lived on the second floor, the most comfortable floor to live on. Brother places great emphasis on women's sports, and the women's handball team is strong. They often go off to different prefectures and countries for tournaments and exhibition games. The company recruits heavily for this team and rewards the members for their victories. The handball players are given cushy jobs as receptionists or inspectors on the lines, and they work only from 9:00 to 3:00, leaving early for long practices lasting until 7:00 or 8:00 P.M. The stars of the team become "morale officers" and shout friendly encouragement to the on-line laborers: "You're doing great! Let's keep it up. Good job!" Most of the factory workers appreciate them. It is understood that members of the handball team practice hard and live restricted lives outside of the workplace.

The rest of the women on the second floor were OLs. The rooms were relatively nice, and the tatami mats had recently been replaced. The lobby, dining hall, bath, and instruction rooms were within easy reach. The second floor also had the best automatic washing machine and the building's only Western-style toilet. When I first arrived in Nagoya, I was given a private suite on this floor, but I soon moved to another room on the fourth floor that was more run down. I felt that this gave me a better perspective on the life of the average OL and factory woman in Brother.

One of the other women's teams in the dormitory was the softball team, which also lived on the fourth floor. Many of the players were young and well-known for their antics. They did not win many games and received little recognition in terms of relaxed rules and working hours. Like the handball players, they kept their hair cropped short so they looked—as they described it—like boys. The softball team did not take winning as seriously as the handball players, who reaped actual company benefits for their intense training and their many victories. The softball team only practiced from 6:00 to 9:00 P.M., Monday to Saturday. After practice, they ate dinner in big groups, told jokes about the girls in their group, and laughed out loud. Since they looked like boys, they acted the part and frequently told other women in the company that they looked especially cute that day, and asked if they had dates. They also tried to mimic ballet dancers on the dining room stage during special dormitory ceremonies, sending everyone into fits of laughter. Members of the softball team enjoyed coming into my room to ask about America or to tease me about my funny-looking American toothpaste and shampoo, with "English written all over everything."

OLs and factory women lived on the third, fourth, and fifth floors of Aoi dormitory. The fifth floor was almost exclusively factory women. A community of six deaf women in their late twenties lived on the seventh floor, isolated from the rest of the women. The deaf women worked in the factories since the noisy machines did not bother them. They communicated with each other in sign language, and with the other women with gestures and facial expressions. The deaf women will probably remain in Aoi dormitory until they are twenty-nine, when they must move into apartments of their own.

They will probably stay in the factory, as it is difficult for them to find another job or to find a husband. With their handicap, they are considered "imperfect" by Nagoya standards and therefore unlikely to marry.

No one lived on the eighth floor, where the dormitory piano and the rarely used study rooms were located. These rooms are kept locked between the hours of 10:00 P.M. and 6:00 A.M.

The character of each floor of the dormitory changes slightly every six months, when the supervisor announces new rooming assignments. This is necessary since the dormitory has a high attrition rate. Chika, an on-line factory woman, commented: "They just put you with people who they know that you won't get along with. I like to watch television and go to bed late, and they've matched me with a woman who goes to bed early, gets up early, and never wants to do anything after work." A few of the rooming groups that I observed did get along well, but most of the women were indifferent to or had no special affection for the women they lived with. As with crowding, some rooming assignments make dormitory life uncomfortable and encourage early marriage.

The company acts as a stereotypical strong-willed Japanese father. Women have no choice but to remain quiet and accept all of the changes it imposes. The presence of the company is inescapable. The large brass characters on the outer gates spell out the company name. The walls of the lobby are covered with posters of new Brother products or companywide events. All of the microwaves, laundry machines, sewing and knitting machines, pianos, irons, and desks are Brother products. Women must follow the rules of company life or leave the dormitory.

In assuming a paternal role, the company tries to create a community that will look after the young women until they marry and leave the dormitory. It all begins with a ceremony. All new residents are initiated into dormitory life in April. The personnel division welcomes freshmen to Aoi dormitory and introduces them to the management. Afterward, everyone sings two versions of the company song, "Seishun no uta" (Song of Youth), eats cheap sushi, and drinks Fanta orange soda. New residents receive a handbook that introduces them to dormitory life. Entitled "Happy Dormitory Life," this forty-four-page pamphlet covers almost every aspect of dormitory life in minute detail. An old photograph, taken about the time the building was first built, adorns the front cover and shows the dorm in a rosy light. The barbed wire is not visible. The bushes surrounding the building have just been planted, and they do not conceal the building as they do now. Next to the building is an empty lot, where now stands a large apartment building.

The Brother "Songs of Youth" appear on the first and last pages of the handbook, respectively. "Song of Youth (I)" (figure 1) reads:

Kimi o sasotte	I invite you
Machi yukeba	If we go to town
Wakai kokoro ni	May the dreams in our
Yume o yobu	young hearts be realized
Buraza-mishin no—	Ah—That neon sign
Ano neon—a—	of Brother Sewing Machines
Hitomi o agete	Raise your eyes
Mayu o agete	Raise your eyebrows
Uta oshanai ka	Shan't we sing?
Boku to anata to	Mine and yours and
Anato to boku no	Yours and mine
Ra ra ra wakodo no uta	La la la our song of youth
Kimi no te o tori	If I took your hand and we
Tabi sureba	traveled past train windows
Kisha no mado kara	The letters of Brother
Tonde kuru	Sewing Machines
Buraza-mishin no	Would come flying by
Ano moji yo—a—	The letters—ah—
Kiteki no oto mo	The sounds of the whistle

Hassunderu	pierce the air
Akarui rizu-mu	Bright rhythms
Boku to anata to	Mine and yours and
Anata to Boku no	Yours and mine
Ra ra ra wakodo no uta	La la la our song of youth
Kimi to umibe no	If I stand and look
Oka ni tachi mireba	On the shores with you,
Oki-yuku yotto ni mo	On a big yacht we'll see
Buraza-mishin mo	The mark of Brother
Ano ma-ku—a—	Sewing Machines—ah—
Shioji ni	To these characters
Saita shiro bara ni	To blooming white roses
Todokeyo uta yo	Let's deliver this song
Boku to anata to	Mine and yours and
Anata to boku no	Yours and mine
Ra ra ra wakodo no uta	La la la our song of youth

This song is full of the imagery of youth and energy. *Seishun* refers not only to youth but to "springtime, the prime of life." It stirs up visions of flowers blooming and of young men and women at the peak of adolescence, growing into adulthood. Brother views its young female laborers as "blooming white roses" with "young hearts" who need to be molded into outstanding young adults. It views itself as an innovative international company that is responsible for the psychological and ethical maturity of its naive young women workers. Nevertheless, few women freely sing the songs of youth, or view the company as a major factor in their maturation.

Aoi dormitory tries to create an environment of paternalism, an extension of the family group, to facilitate this passage from girlhood into womanhood. Drawings from a Brother recruitment leaflet, entitled "Handmade Youth," illustrate the company's intentions (figure 2). At age eighteen, girls graduate from high school and adjust to their first year of adult life. The leaflet states: "Now

Figure 1. Brother "Song of Youth (I)"

Figure 2. **"Handmade Youth," Brother recruitment pamphlet**

In what manner will you ascend the steps of youth?

21
It's a little early but you reached your "goal in." Your savings are very helpful.

20
You move one step up. It is expected that you will come across a "stunning steady" and...

19
Education continues after graduation. Suddenly it seems that you have become ladylike.

18
Now you are both an adult and a student. You have good memories of campus life.

you are both an adult and a student. You have good memories of campus life." At nineteen, the girl prepares for marriage by undergoing bridal training. She takes special classes offered to the dormitory residents, in which she studies traditional Japanese arts and wifely skills—cooking, sewing, knitting. The caption states: "Education continues after graduation. Suddenly it seems that you have become 'ladylike' [*onnarashi*, 'a woman as a woman should be')." At age twenty, the woman dates. The caption reads: "At age twenty, you move one step up. It is expected that you will come across a 'stunning steady' and ... " By age twenty-one, she is at the altar and has completed her life course. She leaves the company. The woman in the cartoon has stepped off the rising pedestal. The caption says: "It's a little early but you reached your 'goal in' [i.e., got married]. Your savings are very helpful."

With such a recruitment leaflet, the Brother personnel division tries to attract women who wish to work for a few years, marry, and then leave the company. This leaflet projects the same image of happy adolescence as that of the Brother "Songs of Youth." A bright photograph of a young girl's hand-sewn pocketbook embroidered with the sentence "I love Brother" adorns the cover. Surrounding this pocketbook are a small fern, a cup of coffee, an old-fashioned tin of candies, and a modern stationery set. In the background is an orange, red, blue, and green tablecloth. The picture mixes domestic and high-tech elements yet remains feminine, with the sprinkling of flowers and polka dots in the design. It projects an impression of home and warmth to appeal to the young adolescents who are reluctant to leave the family nest.

The different sections of this pamphlet are referred to as "lessons." The first lesson is entitled "Thanks, Adolescence." A photograph of Keiko (the prototypical Brother female employee) takes up most of this two-page lesson. Keiko, beaming with health, is attired in tennis wear. It is a sunny day and she plays happily on the company tennis team. A letter from Keiko's friend appears above the picture, expressing how amazed she is that Keiko has become a Brother lady, and how wonderful it is that she is having so much fun playing tennis. The friend notes, "I guess it's time to figure out the course of your life. You won't go on to college (because you're having so much fun) . . . you must be extremely thankful. The people in your workplace, your senior workers, the dormitory supervisor and his wife, the company group, have really come to your assistance. You are probably saying, 'Thank you, youth.' I'm so happy that you have joined the group."

A cartoon appears to the side of the letter. This cartoon, like many of the other pictures in the pamphlet, is a caricature of a young girl in an affected feminine pose. Many of the cartoon women who fill the pages of this pamphlet hold their hands up to their chins, blushing shyly. They all have large blue eyes, brown hair, pink cheeks, tiny red lips, and either heart-shaped or round faces. The idealized cartoon figures of young Brother employees are shown frolicking in mountain pastures with young boys and cows, painting pictures, receiving archery, guitar, or yachting lessons, and traveling to foreign countries.

In this idealized picture, Brother presents itself as a "finishing school." It promises to mold young women from distant prefectures into tennis players, archery experts, and likely brides. Most of the women at Brother do not, of course, become skilled mountaineers or artists. The women entering the company are attracted by these promises, yet they are realistic and know that the promises will probably not be met. They understand that the company fulfills a social function on another level, through the dormitory classes in bridal training. These popular classes meet once a week and cost two thousand yen (sixteen dollars) for two months of instruction and all materials. Women who master the sewing, knitting, cooking, tea ceremony, and flower arranging skills may actually increase their prospects for marriage. Many residents of Brother's male dormitories whom I interviewed said they wanted wives who could cook very well and were trained in such wifely skills.

Residents of women's dormitories are commonly known to be chaste. The physical barriers discussed in this chapter stand as a symbol of the company's attitude toward women's morality. It is generally thought that virgins make more desirable marriage partners than sexually experienced young women, to understate the case.

The dormitory assures that its women are chaste by setting up social as well as physical barriers. One of these is the group. Women who enter the dormitory belong to the group of residents. The preface of the Aoi dormitory pamphlet introduces this notion. It reads, "We are very happy to introduce you to the group." The introduction goes on to express the joys of membership in the dormitory clique: "We who work in this company walk smiling with pride and self-confidence in our breasts." It is difficult for a woman to be independent while she conforms to her group. Lacking independence, she will probably stay out of trouble.

To join the group and to enjoy the rewards of participation, residents must follow the rules, which are an effective method for controlling young Japanese women. The pamphlet states: "We would like everyone to live a happy, bright, and healthy dormitory life by correctly following the rules." Life in Aoi dormitory is completely regulated, as rules govern all aspects of life: bathing, eating, personal habits, and access to the dormitory.

Even communication with the outside world is regulated. Women may receive phone calls on three community phones in the dorm office from 6:00 P.M. to 10:00 P.M. All calls are received under the watchful eyes of the dormitory management. Anyone wishing to call out may use one of the ten pay phones in the lobby, which stays lit until 10:30 P.M. The pay telephones may be used twenty-four hours a day, but the women cannot receive calls at these phones, and if they make calls at irregular hours they will have to talk in the dark.

Bathing times are limited to 7:00 P.M. to 10:30 P.M. With many people bathing at the same time, group consciousness is fostered. The pink-tiled bathroom has fifty showerheads, evenly spaced around the room, and two large metal bathtubs. Each tub has a capacity of thirty women. The older sisters turn on the hot water to fill the tubs. Rooming groups assigned to monitor the bathroom turn off the hot water at 10:30 and clean the tubs, the shelves, and the showerheads. The dormitory management keeps the doors locked during off hours.

Women take baths in seemingly organized groups. The factory women prefer to bathe at 7:00 P.M. when they get home. They are exhausted, and they wash away the grime that has accumulated from a day of handling greasy machine parts. The factory women who don't bathe at this time are preoccupied with other activities— classes in cooking, flower arrangement, or television. OLs wander in around 8:00 or 9:00 P.M. The handball team usually bathes after practice and dinner at 9:00. The softball team always comes down to the bath at 10:00.

The bathroom door is made of smoky glass and metal. The Japanese characters for bath (*furo*) are taped onto the door. Rows of wooden shelves stand by the entrance. Placing their dormitory slippers on these shelves, the girls ascend into the dressing room floor in their bare feet. The floor is carpeted with material resembling astroturf. Wooden, boxlike shelves at the far end of the room hold clothing. Two full-length mirrors stand to the right. Bathroom scales, each with a physical evaluation chart, are on the floor. The scales indicate whether one is too thin, just right, fat, or grossly fat. Women are very conscious of their weight and appearance, and most aspire to rakelike thinness. Slimmer girls seem more likely to attract the stunning fiancé drawn in the Brother recruitment manual.

The women put their clothes on the wooden shelves and carry plastic basins filled with soap, shampoo, creme rinse, and wash-cloths into the adjoining room. Picking up a plastic stool at the entrance, they sit down in front of a showerhead. After a twenty-minute wash and shower of the entire body, the women soak in the steaming hot water of the tub. This is a peaceful and relaxing time for most women, except when the playful softball players are there. They uphold their reputation for silliness by singing at the tops of their lungs and pushing each other around the tub.

The strictest rule for Brother dormitory residents is the curfew. Those who come home after 9:30 P.M. are punished. Ten minutes of tardiness results in a week of washing the lobby windows or the bathrooms at 6:00 A.M., or an equivalent chore; thirty minutes, in two weeks of chores. These cleaning duties are in addition to the regular duties assigned monthly to different rooming groups.

With special permission and two weeks' notice, women can leave the dorm for a night. A detailed form must be filled out explaining where the woman will be, and giving telephone numbers where she can be contacted. Permission for an overnight leave is granted only if the proper forms have been completed. Leaving without permission results in severe punishment—grounding for a month. The grounded woman cannot leave on the weekends and has to come home directly from work. These rules were much more severe before I arrived. Previously the dormitory supervisor noti-fied the woman's parents of her intended overnight leave. If the parents did not consent, the leave was denied. In the past two years, the rules have become more lax. The women plan ahead, fill out the proper forms, giving the telephone numbers and addresses of friends in the city, and go to discos or clubs and stay at a friend's apartment, or in a cheap capsule hotel in Nagoya. Parental permission is no longer required.

Aside from the curfews, there are restrictions on many of the general use rooms. The laundry rooms, kitchens, instruction rooms, study rooms, and music rooms are locked every night from 10:00 until 6:00 A.M. This results in long lines for the washing machines early in the day. Women who want to boil water for tea have to do so before 10:00 P.M. I suppose that this is done, in part, for reasons of safety. The dormitory supervisor sleeps from 10:00 until 6:00 and expects the women to rest at that time too. Turning off the power in the laundry rooms and locking the kitchens also saves energy. One factory woman complained, however, "These rules are ridiculous. I wish the laundry rooms were open all of the time. Sometimes, I don't have the time to do all of my laundry." The supervisor of the men's dormitories keeps all of the rooms open twenty-four hours a day. The personnel department feels that since the men have to work until 2:00 or 3:00 A.M. during the company's busiest times, they should not be subjected to restrictions on laundry facilities, the bath, kitchens, or curfew. On the other hand, women are not expected to work late, or to stay out late.

Other prohibitions are unwritten. Women are told the first week that they must not smoke cigarettes or bring cars to the dormitory. Parking space is provided for the residents of the men's dormitories, but women are discouraged from the unladylike practice of owning a car. Drinking is acceptable for residents, as long as it is done outside the dormitory. Most of the residents frown upon drunkenness, inside or outside the dorm. In a conversation between two young factory women, one said to the other, "You drank too much in Tsubohachi [the local pub] and were talking loudly. It was embarrassing. You sounded like you were scolding everyone."

Although many of the salarymen keep stashes of alcohol in their dormitory rooms or buy beer from vending machines on the way back to their dormitories, the women do not. I was given bottles of beer and Bailey's Irish Cream at an import fair. Naively, I offered to share them with some of the women at my dormitory. Not one of them accepted; they all felt that drinking in the dormitory was wrong.

There are strict guidelines concerning meals as well. Women order their meals in advance and can only go to the dining halls during specified hours of the day. At dinner, they can buy snacks and sundries at a small stand in the dining hall. The company sells food that is left over from lunch, snack foods, and toiletries at the small store. The residents buy snacks and bring them to their rooms to eat with friends after their bath or to supplement their dinners. Most women sit up until midnight in their rooms, watching television or talking about people in their work sections. The conversations I took part in were usually light and humorous. The women, some wearing brown or green mudpacks on their faces, sat around the coffee tables eating rice crackers, drinking tea, sometimes talking about their boyfriends or fiancés. As the night drew on, they went off to their beds.

Brother Industries—as the guardian of these women—believes it has to uphold their moral and physical well-being inside and outside the workplace. The dormitory is designed to be the second home of the young women from regions of Japan too far away to commute on a daily basis. The strict rules and the bridal training classes assure parents that their daughters will be well taken care of. The director of Brother personnel stated in a recent discussion with the directors of other industries on the changing roles of women that "Women will leave the company to fulfill their roles as housewives and mothers. That is why it is difficult to give them equal treatment." This spirit underlies most of the Aoi dormitory policies.

CHAPTER FIVE

Portraits of Hardship

DURING THE COURSE of my internship at Brother, I conducted formal interviews with more than forty factory women and office ladies and made friends with even more. This chapter focuses on the lives of two types of women: those who followed the expected life course of female workers, and those who, for some reason or other, chose not to. The reasons they give highlight some of the difficulties faced by women workers in Japan.

Sachiyo, Mari, Tomoko, Naomi, and Keiko are all factory women. Sachiyo and Mari make typewriters. They joined the company in different years, after leaving junior high school. Both thought that they would work in the factory for several years before getting married. Two years after joining the company, Mari was engaged. Sachiyo has worked on the line for fifteen years with little hope for change. Tomoko is married, yet she remains on the line. She lives a dual life: at home, she is a housewife and mother; at the company, she sticks labels onto finished typewriters. Naomi works to support her family and to put herself through night school, where she is working toward her high school diploma. Keiko is a senior worker in the company and oversees productivity on the line. She is a career woman in a company that makes no provisions for women who remain employed indefinitely. At age thirty-one, she no longer sees marriage as a viable option.

The office ladies discussed below also represent a wide spectrum of interests and characteristics. They are Reiko, Miyuki, Etsuko, Hitomi, and An Ping. Reiko, who entered the company after graduating from college, rents an apartment with her younger sister. She would like to marry and leave what she calls the "underpaid" OL life. Miyuki was an OL until June 1986 when she married a young salesman in the company. After they were transferred to the United States, she became a housewife there. Etsuko, Hitomi, and An Ping were OLs who left the company because their intentions clashed with those of their supervisors. An Ping, a twenty-four-year-old Taiwanese, was the only full-time non-Japanese OL ever hired by the company.

Before the interviews, I told the women that they would remain anonymous. I have changed their names and the places where they lived to preserve this confidence.

The Factory Women

Sachiyo

Sachiyo's shyness struck a chord in me when I met her. She seemed somewhat melancholy when she intimated her feelings and traced out the events in her life. We talked on a worn wooden bench with chipping, dirty green paint, at the far end of the factory. The sounds of clanking metal parts resounded in our ears. Sachiyo is tall and slender and incredibly soft-spoken. At times, the background noise drowned out what she said—her voice was nearly a whisper. Sitting down, she stared at her shoes and did not raise her head until I said something that provoked her. Then, she glared at me in surprise for a second or two for my boldness before diverting her eyes.

The first question that disturbed her was when I asked her age. She refused to tell me exactly but revealed that she began work in the factory fifteen years ago, before finishing junior high school. This allowed me to approximate her age at roughly twenty-six to twenty-eight years. (Junior high school students are usually eleven to fourteen years of age. Adding fifteen years to these figures yields twenty-six to twenty-nine years. Sachiyo still lives in the dormitory, a privilege allowed only to women twenty-eight years old or younger.) Sachiyo feels that she has let the ''marriageable'' years slip by her and says that she has ''no confidence in her own hope for marriage.'' She has even resorted to *omiai*, arranged introductions to prospective marriage partners, but to no avail. She says it's ''too difficult to find someone she likes.'' She no longer works for her dowry but for what she refers to as ''money for emergencies and times of need.''

Sachiyo looked up at me when I asked about her family. She works to alleviate the financial burden on her family. She and her brother, a salaryman in a small company, support themselves, trying not to be the stereotypical *kuchiberashi* (grain wasters), children in traditional Japan who remained in the home, did not support themselves, and ate away the family fortune. Her parents' home, where she grew up, is too far away in Aichi Prefecture for her to commute daily. Sachiyo's father drives a bus, and her mother does clerical work in a local firm. They have their own working and social lives, quite separate from those of their children. Sachiyo has become somewhat of a loner. She dropped out of junior high school because she ''hated to study and wanted to work.'' She always dreamed of a fashion-related job or some ''glamorous'' OL job, but she needed to help her family by becoming financially independent.

As the first woman on the line, Sachiyo takes the typewriter chassis that come flowing off the robot lines and places them on the line for the workers. She positions motors and drills them onto the chassis with a power drill. She has been doing the same thing for over a decade. She commented: ''I find work very difficult. The overtime hours are especially hard. But I think that I've gotten used to it. It really doesn't bother me anymore.'' If her family were rich, she says that she ''would like to travel and not work.'' Like many other factory women, she watches television for recreation and would like to visit many of the places that appear in the programs. She also hopes for something better, although she believes that her wishes are unattainable.

Sachiyo's responses are typical of many of the women who come to the company to work and do not find a husband before they reach the so-called marriageable age—up to approximately twenty-five or twenty-six. These women express similar feelings of helplessness. Many lost either one or both parents in their childhood or have suffered some other adversity. Women who have experienced great losses are stronger in spirit and less willing to compromise with unsuitable omiai matches. They have high standards for marriage partners, and unlike many of the younger women, they do not believe that a bad marriage is a suitable alternative to the drudgery of working life. They also want to help their parents more. As adults, they feel that it is not right to live at home and to depend on their parents, who are struggling to support themselves.

Looking at Sachiyo, I discovered that it is not merely experience that makes one a senior worker. After fifteen years in the same work group, Sachiyo has not become a senior worker because she lacks desire and the proper attitude to lead. The factory, which has provided her with a means for subsistence, has also been a continuation of her hardships. Unwilling to compromise on an unhappy marriage, and no longer considered to be marriageable by social standards, she has no alternative but to stay in the factory or to find some other menial job. Her recognition that she will be a spinster in a society where women are expected to marry, and her daily grind in the factory, have effectively killed her spirit.

Mari

Mari, a twenty-one-year-old worker on the subline, entered the company after graduating from high school. She sees herself as part of the turnover process of female workers, in which young women join the line, work for several years, and then leave the company to marry. The company can then replace them with a fresh new crop of young workers. She said: "I joined this line with five other women. So far, everyone has married and left. Only I am left. I will marry next year and leave the company too. There will be new people here."

Mari rides the train for one hour every morning to get to work from her home in Aichi Prefecture. She has an older brother and a sister. Her father is a sanitation worker for the city of Nagoya, and her mother works in a small industry where she spins thread from cotton. Mari is engaged to be married to a clerk in a small company. She is saving up to pay for the wedding ceremony and for her dowry.

Mari reflected on line work: "It's all very tiring. I wouldn't mind changing jobs, but I have saved a lot of money. I'm saving for my dowry. After a year, I should have enough money. Then, I'll quit." She wants shorter working hours, longer rest periods, and no overtime. She added, "I found this company in the classified section of the newspaper. I picked it up because it offered a lot of vacation days. I want to be a housewife until the children have all grown up. Then, I'll look for another job."

Mari is happy as a factory worker. Perhaps this is because she knows that her job is temporary, and she has marriage to look forward to. She said, "I look at OLs and I'm glad that I'm not working in an office. OLs are confined to their desks. The section chief gives them a lot of orders. We factory women can use our bodies and our hands. They just sit there and take orders." Most factory women whom I interviewed were reluctant to become OLs, even if given the chance. Perhaps they were rationalizing their low positions in the company, and this helped them deal with the hardships in their lives. Yet they felt a certain dignity in working in the factory, and they were glad to have a small degree of independence. They were not subject to constant orders from superiors.

Mari represents what the personnel division sees as the model woman worker. Factory work has eroded some of her spirit and energy, but she does it to serve a greater end, marriage. This goal is expedient for the company, and it helps Mari endure her daily hardships much better than the others. In contrast, Sachiyo and other women who remain in the factory past the marriageable age find themselves in an unfavorable situation: they are stuck in a menial job with little hope of a change.

Tomoko

Tomoko is one of only two married women on the subline. The other, Tomita, is a senior worker with no children who remains on the line to make extra money for herself and her husband. Tomoko, at twenty-two, is too young to be a line supervisor like Tomita, and she also lacks the ambition or the proper leadership qualities for the job. Tomoko is one of the more unusual factory women. She has a daughter who she leaves under the watchful eyes of her mother at 6:30 every morning when she commutes to work with her husband, a factory worker in the sewing machine division. Tomoko hurries home each evening to cook dinner and do housework.

She met her husband three years ago through mutual friends in the company. At the age of twenty she married, much to her "disbelief." She said that she met her husband at a party, fell in love, and married him. Tomoko had her baby when she was twenty-one years old. Needless to say, life for her has not been easy, although she seems to have fulfilled the social expectations of marriage and children. She feels as though youth has slipped away from her. She recalled: "One minute, I was playing on the badminton team in high school with all of the girls. The next minute, I was married and had a daughter. I don't regret it at all. My husband is a good man, a bit stuck up at times, but basically a good person. But really, I can't believe that I'm actually married." She didn't want to lose him at the time he proposed; it was sooner than she had wanted to get married, but she jumped at the chance. She is grateful that her mother is willing to take care of her daughter, and that she can leave her child with her when she participates in after-hours activities with other factory women.

Tomoko dislikes factory work but worries about her family's finances. She finds it difficult to save. "My husband's salary," she said, "is too low to support four people. I make money for the family too. I want to save for family travel but it's impossible." Tomoko wishes that she could spend more time with her daughter at home, but she must support her family. She remarked, "I want things to be better for my children, so they can have all of the things that I couldn't. I want them to go to foreign countries and to learn different things. I have no time for myself. I want them to be able to enjoy different things." Tomoko aspires to be an ideal mother. She understands that a mother's role in her society is one of sacrifice. Although she indulges in some amusements with her friends, for the most part her life is one of labor, at work and in the home. Her happiness derives from that of her family, especially her child.

After graduating from an all-girl high school in Aichi Prefecture, Tomoko looked for a job in the confectionary business without success. She found work at Brother. With her education and lack of experience, she resigned herself to being a line worker. She was attracted by the friendliness of the people, by the many vacation days, and by the company's prestige. She wanted a job in which she could use her hands. She feels that she has gained much practical experience as an adult; she has married and had children. Nonetheless, although she has fulfilled the social expectation of marriage, Tomoko cannot yet enjoy the benefits of being a wife. She married for love and chose a man who could not support a family on his own. Her family cannot survive if she does not work. The other women on the line look up to her. Some day they will marry and have children too, but, unlike Tomoko, most will quit their jobs.

Naomi

Naomi has worked in the factory for six years. She lives with her parents and brother about one mile from the factory and rides her bicycle to work. Her mother answers phones in a small bakery. Naomi is slightly embarrassed that her mother must work to support her family. Her brother works in a printing company. She rarely sees her father, who drives trucks across Japan.

At twenty, Naomi is one of the prize workers of the line. She is energetic and works hard without showing any sign of fatigue, as typewriters have become second nature to her. She does the final inspection of the finished typewriters before they are sent off to the packing department. Naomi is shorter than the other women; she stands on a box to do her work on the line and yells encouragement to the other workers in a high-pitched voice that can be heard above the rest. Her hair is permed in short, tight curls, and she wears striking purple eye shadow that seems to match her energetic personality.

The personnel division asked Naomi to teach the fundamentals of typewriter manufacture to employees at the new company plant in Switzerland. The date for her departure was not set in 1987 when I spoke to her. She was eager to leave Japan, and she spent her days dreaming about it.

Unlike many of the other factory workers, Naomi loves to study. She very much wanted to go to high school, but her parents could not afford it; they told her she must pay her own way. She pursues a dream of being a kindergarten teacher and is earning her high school diploma by going to night school near the factory. Naomi gives half of her savings to her mother and keeps the other half for herself. She says that she is saving for travel and to buy some nice things for herself.

Naomi is very young; as she put it, "too young for marriage." She has not given any real thought to saving for her dowry. She said confidently, "I want to marry at twenty-five, but before that I want to go to Switzerland. I am saving money to travel, and I want to have a lot of different experiences before I marry." Naomi knows that once she marries, she will have few chances to travel, and perhaps no opportunity to go abroad.

One night Naomi took me to her night school. Work ended at 6:00 P.M. We changed out of our uniforms into street clothes. It took ten minutes to drive from the factory to the school, where we parked in a lot full of student cars and motorcycles. Young factory workers, fishermen, clerks, and other workers arrived at 7:00. It was already dark. The students ate boxed dinners while listening attentively to the teacher's lectures. Classes went on until 10:00, at which time Naomi went to rehearsal for one of the school's theatrical productions. She usually got home at midnight, slept until 7:00 A.M., and started a new day of work at the factory.

I spoke to Naomi's English teacher, Okamoto, about her. He said: "Naomi's one of the brighter ones. I think that she might get an interesting job somewhere. I'm afraid that the others don't have great aspirations. They have no confidence and they are unsure of their abilities. They tell themselves that they can't learn. They try hard but get discouraged and end up in the same jobs that they started off with." Okamoto believes that the students who attend night school could do more with their education. Many of them struggle with English and other subjects to make up for the inadequacies in their education. They enrolled because they wanted to be there or because they could increase their salaries with the extra degree, yet, for many of them, the latter was not a consideration. Okamoto was sad to see that higher education did not improve their lives.

Naomi, I felt, was a student with confidence. Nevertheless, this confidence and independence mayultimately be detrimental to her chances for finding a marriage partner. She seems to be more interested in developing her career than in marriage—most of the other women her age are already thinking about becoming wives. The men in the company are not interested in strong-willed women who clearly state their own opinions. Naomi will probably become a kindergarten teacher, one who has traveled to Switzerland. Yet she, like Sachiyo, may be doomed to be a spinster.

Keiko

Keiko was born in 1956 in Nara Prefecture, where she spent the first eighteen years of her life. Her father was what she described as a "day laborer." He never had steady work but managed to keep the family going by doing odd jobs in homes or on farms for a fee. Her mother, who was a housewife, died shortly after Keiko finished high school. Keiko took on her mother's responsibilities, cleaning the house, preparing meals, and watching over her younger brother. When she was seventeen, she landed a job as a clerk in the town office of her village.

She wanted to leave Nara to see what life was like in another prefecture. She found the perfect opportunity when she saw in the newspaper a classified ad for Brother Industries, a company far from Nara. She hoped to become an OL, but with her limited education, the personnel division felt that she was better suited for assembly line work. Keiko left her family and was placed on the subline in the typewriter factory. She lived in Aoi dormitory for five years until she could not stand it anymore. She said, "I was already twenty-three. I wanted to live alone. The rules are silly. They were written for little girls, not for young women." She moved into an apartment near the factory eight years ago and has lived there ever since.

Keiko is now thirty-one years old. She no longer assembles typewriters but works on the side, keeping inventory on production, and on the different models of typewriters that this line produces. Her other responsibility is quality control. Keiko plans to work in the factory for many more years. She gave up the idea of marriage at the age of thirty. She said, "I'd love to have children but I just don't want to get married anymore. I've been independent for so long that I've gotten used to it. I think that I'll be here for a long time. The problem is that men's and women's jobs are so different. Men are taught engineering and design so they advance in their jobs. It's different for women." Keiko noted that the content of women's jobs rarely changes, no matter how long they work at the company.

Keiko said that she spends her free time with friends from the workplace. She takes lessons in kimono making, and she wants to learn English conversation. If she were ever to get rich, she would send money to her father and go somewhere with open space, like Hokkaido. Keiko is concerned about her job at the company. As a final comment, she said, "I've been here for a long time. When I started work here, we usually worked six days a week. Now things have changed. I was here through the rough times in the company. Sometimes, girls were let go. Companies can be very selfish. I wonder if they may send me out sometime too."

Although Keiko has survived the company lay-offs, she wonders how long she will be able to take the hardships and tedium of factory work. But she believes that at her age, she will be unable to find a husband who can support her. She refuses to compromise on a marriage that is less than ideal; she would rather live alone, remaining in the factory for as long as she is allowed, or as long as she physically can. Keiko is one of the exceptional factory women who, contrary to expectations, remain single and make factory work their career.

The Office Ladies

Reiko

Reiko was born on a small farm at the foot of a mountain in Gero, a rural town in Gifu Prefecture. Her father is a clerk in the Gero town office; her mother, the head nurse in the local hospital. Her older sister teaches at the nursery school in town. After graduating from a junior college for women in Nagoya with a degree in home economics, Reiko became an OL at Brother. She said, "The pay is not so good but it's all right. I had a little apartment in Nagoya that I used during my junior college years. I joined this company because it was easy to get to from where I live." After graduating from college, Reiko wanted to leave the farm and experience living and working by herself. She stayed in her small apartment because she did not think that she could conform easily to the strict rules of the dormitory.

Reiko is twenty-two years old. She does not enjoy the daily routine of OL life but ''cannot find a more interesting job that pays the rent.'' In the planning office of the Brother Sales company, she photocopies relevant articles from newspapers and business journals and answers telephone calls and letters for her bosses. Sometimes she draws diagrams and figures on the marker boards for meetings. Reiko had been at Brother for two years when I first came to the office. She takes her work light-heartedly, spending her mornings boiling water for tea and chatting with the other OLs before the bosses arrive. There is an established hierarchy of OLs in the office. The bosses give the most challenging jobs to the graduates of Japan's most prestigious colleges. Reiko graduated without distinction from a local women's college, and, as a result, most of her work is clerical and unchallenging.

Reiko invited me to spend a three-day weekend with her family in Gero. They own a large, fifty-year-old wooden farmhouse in the mountains, and the small hill on which their house sits. Her ancestors have lived there for centuries, growing rice and vegetables. Reiko's grandmother does the farming on the tilled sections of land. Her grandfather raises carp in the small pond to the side of the house. Her grandparents, now in their seventies, seldom leave their large old home in Gero. They speak a rural form of Japanese, which Reiko said most people from places outside Gero do not understand. But they understand the standard Japanese that Reiko uses to speak to them.

This family has maintained its traditional ways. The father and uncle leave work early to catch fish in the nearby river for their dinner table. There are no locks on their doors and no running water in their home. They get water from a stream that flows from the mountains. On summer nights, the dining room is filled with insects, flying over everyone's heads, and Reiko and her sisters run outside to catch fireflies. They have one cow and a rooster that crows at the crack of dawn. Yet, like most farm families, they cannot support themselves by farming alone. Everyone must do their share of chores around the farm after work or on weekends.

Most of Reiko's friends from the village high school are OLs, salarymen, or college students. Many, like Reiko, have left the village for Tokyo, Osaka, or Nagoya, yet they get together during extended company or school holidays in coffee shops in the heart of the village where they drink beers and tell jokes. Unlike some of her friends, Reiko did not enroll in a four-year college because she "hated studying." She liked the relaxed pace of life on the farm, but she wanted to live in a big, exciting city. She considered moving to Tokyo but felt that it was too big and too far away from home. She settled on Nagoya, a good compromise between the relaxed life of Gero and the intensity of Tokyo.

She hoped to become an OL or a fashion designer after graduating from junior college. (Becoming a fashion designer was a common dream of many OLs whom I interviewed.) She had no experience in the fashion world and found the OL route to be the most feasible at the time. She still dreams of fashion design and takes classes in sewing on Wednesday nights in one of the Nagoya culture centers. She is not sure if she is talented enough to be a successful designer, and she would never quit her job to pursue this dream. Reiko is afraid of failing and feels the need to support herself financially, at least until she marries. The other OLs in her work section comprise her group of friends in Nagoya. She shops with them after work and goes to discos with them on Friday and Saturday nights—her favorite recreation, outside of making clothes. This gives her a chance to wear less conservative clothes and to be seen at Nagoya's most fashionable spots. She acts very differently at the office, where she never talks about her personal life. She warned me: "In the office, you can't talk about things like discos." The other OLs agree. They are conscious of the impression they would make on the salarymen in the office. They believe that such talk would make their male coworkers think that they were immoral or not serious about their work. They are afraid that such knowledge would upset the relationships in the office and encourage coworkers to gossip about them and to lose respect for them.

Reiko shares her small apartment with her younger sister, who also graduated from junior college and waits tables in a Nagoya family restaurant. They split the rent. Reiko has a boyfriend but says that she would not consider marrying him or spending the rest of her life with him. She says they "don't get along." She does expect to marry and to leave the company when the right person comes along. She dreams of moving to America where she can have a career. She is saddened by the prospect of becoming a housewife in Japan and spending the rest of her days taking care of children and a husband, but she sees no feasible alternatives. She was thinking about saving for her dowry when I last spoke to her in 1987. Reiko said, "I just break even every month with what I make. There is nothing left for my savings. I'd like to marry at twenty-five or twenty-six when I have more money, but there isn't anyone that I like right now. I think my parents will help me out with the money."

Miyuki

Miyuki was one of the top OLs in her workplace hierarchy. She graduated with a bachelor's degree from Nara Women's University, one of Japan's most prestigious women's colleges. She spent the summer vacation of her senior year traveling the Silk Road in China. She even considered going to graduate school but in the end settled for Brother Industries. She explained, "Women who go to graduate school can't find jobs in industry. By the time they get out of school, they're too old and nobody wants to hire them." At Brother, she had received considerable responsibility as an analyst for the marketing research division, where the personnel department places the "best and brightest" company employees. However, she was still given fewer responsibilities than her male coworkers. Her group did market research and predicted trends, a job indispensable to the success and growth of the company.

Miyuki grew up in Inazawa City in Gifu Prefecture, where her father is a local government official. Her mother is a housewife who has devoted her life to the upkeep and running of her household. Miyuki enjoyed studying and excelled in school, but in spite of her academic successes, her parents told her that a woman's goals in life should be to be a good wife and mother. She said that she accepted this but felt it was bad that women could not be mothers and lead interesting lives at the same time. The accepted view of married life in Nagoya ran against the grain of her attitudes and ambitions in work. She perceived injustice in the assignment of male and female roles in her society but accepted them as a natural part of Japanese life.

In 1987, she married Hiroshi, from Brother Sales, who had been introduced to her three years earlier by her boss, who thought they would make a "good couple." They dated for a year and became engaged. Hiroshi was then sent to the company's New Jersey office for a five-year internship. After two years of a long-distance romance through letters and phone calls, he asked her to marry him and move to the States, where she could keep him company for the remainder of his internship. Miyuki faced a difficult dilemma. She said, "I want to marry some day, but I'm only twenty-four years old, and I don't want to be a housewife now. If I go to the United States, I'll have to quit my job in the marketing research division. I won't be able to get a work visa in America, so I'll have no choice but to stay home."

After much self-reflection and some urging from her fiancé, Miyuki agreed to marriage and retirement. Hiroshi returned to Japan for the wedding, but the couple moved to the United States shortly after they wed. After six months, Miyuki found married life less than ideal. She still wanted to pursue a career. She said, "I really like the United States. Here, the women are free to be mothers and career women. Hiroshi doesn't understand that, and we fight about it all the time. As the wife of a company man, I should also be loyal to the company and help my husband, but I think that being a housewife is too boring.'' Miyuki continues to feel an obligation to serve the company through a transitive vertical relationship. Hiroshi is loyal to the company. Miyuki, the wife, is bound by obligation to her husband and, by extension, to her husband's company.

Marriage between company workers is common at Brother and, in some ways, preferred. It is difficult for the men, who work long hours, to meet women. The bosses sometimes help them by introducing them to women who they think would make good wives. Marriage, they believe, psychologically stabilizes the salaryman and gives him someone who can take care of his needs. The wife—who will be an ex-company worker—will understand the company better than other women and, as a result, be a more supportive companion. Marriage to a company man is also usually good for the woman, as it allows her to stay in touch with her friends in the company and to keep abreast of company events. Yet, for some women, like Miyuki, such benefits may not be very comforting; if given the chance, they would pursue a challenging career and not stay at home.

Etsuko

After attending junior college in Tokyo, Etsuko became an OL at Brother Sales, where she planned the domestic sales of word processors. She demonstrated great promise as an aggressive business woman in her early years at the company and was given many projects throughout the country, but never overseas since the company normally did not send women out of the country (it was felt that being overseas would be ''difficult'' for females). Her male coworkers commented, ''I like having her in the office. She works as hard as any man.'' Even though she worked in the same capacity as a man in her office, Etsuko was obviously not treated like one. She expected no promotions and it was difficult for her to do *settai*, the ''after six'' business transactions conducted over social drinks with clients at a local bar or entertainment spot. Although the men admired her, they also felt threatened by her. One salaryman said, ''I wouldn't want to know her outside of the office. She is too strong-willed and aggressive. Many people are afraid of her.'' Other salarymen expressed similar sentiments. They felt that Etsuko should be more feminine and soft-spoken. It bothered them that she always said what was on her mind and seemed, at times, to be even more aggressive than the men.

Etsuko's strong will comes perhaps from her pride in her background. Her father is a top executive in a local company. Her mother is a locally known and highly skilled tea ceremony and ikebana instructor. Estuko grew up in a large house with much activity; there was constant traffic of students and visiting artists through the main part of the house. Another part of the house was blocked off for the family's boarders, students attending nearby colleges. Etsuko developed an interest in illustrated books and collects children's picture books. Her interest in sports developed after she joined the company women's rugby team, the Hangovers. Supported by her parents, she worked hard at practices and soon became the team's captain. She ran the practices with Sasaki, a forty-five-year-old salaryman who played on rugby teams in his youth and now enjoys coaching the sport. I joined this team in October 1986 to participate and to observe.

Our team met every Sunday in front of the Brother rugby grounds. Etsuko picked me up at 7:45 in front of the dormitory. Sade, Whitney Houston, the Talking Heads, or other popular American music blasted from the stereo in her sports car. We drove to the grounds where we met the other women. The team dressed quickly inside a wooden shack and sat on benches on the perimeter of the field until Sasaki arrived. ''Mama-san,'' a noncompany housewife who had joined the team because she wanted to learn the sport, told jokes while we waited. Beaming with health, Mama-san always spoke lovingly of her husband—who encouraged his wife to play rugby—but said he probably wouldn't be able to handle our tough practices. She brought her two daughters to the practices and the games.

The women on the team identified with Etsuko and Mama-san. They understood that their sport was traditionally male. There were only three women's rugby teams in the country in 1986, and we knew that we were an oddity. A Japanese television network did a documentary on us while I was on the team: they filmed us at practice, putting on makeup before practices, and doing tea cere-mony and things that were considered to be feminine. The TV crew asked us to do all of these things because they wanted to show that we were like all other women in the country, in spite of the fact that we played a typically male sport. But in reality we never put on makeup before a game, and rarely did tea ceremony together. The fact that we were so different from "typical" Japanese women forged strong bonds: we found security in the group.

Etsuko started the practices with the usual exercise regimen: eight arm circles and a detailed routine, the same one at every practice. After the warmups, we practiced throwing the rugby ball. Etsuko divided us into groups. She and I were rugby props, so we practiced plays together. Training on the Nagoya Hangovers was spartan. We were not given water even on the hottest of days until noon, when we drank our fill of the ice-cold barley tea that Mama-san brought to the practices. Etsuko presided over all that happened. Her face red with exhaustion, she waited until the last of her teammates drank tea before she took her first sip. Sometimes we drank beer after our practices or games, which was considered very masculine behavior.

Etsuko, the oldest OL in the planning office, left the company later in 1986. The circumstances surrounding her departure are unclear. The company management reported that she decided to quit her job; Etsuko said that she was fired. Eventually she found a job in a trading company, but she was fired from this post for being too willful and for offering too many of her own opinions. Some of her former coworkers at Brother were not surprised. They understood that certain behavior, acceptable for men in the office, is absolutely not permitted for women. Etsuko then retired to home life and studied tea ceremony and flower arrangement with her mother. Becoming more soft-spoken, she was able to meet and marry a salaryman from the Dai Ichi Kangyo Bank. She is now a mother and a full-time housewife.

Hitomi

Hitomi also left the company. She was not willful; her boss in the advertising division had been a "tyrant." One of her OL colleagues left, and her boss gave all of that woman's responsibilities to Hitomi in addition to her regular duties. Hitomi worked long hours, from 8:00 A.M. to 9:00 P.M., to complete her work. Her boss showed no special appreciation or sympathy toward her. Instead, he treated her as if she were insignificant. Speaking to her, he used the most informal language, as if he were addressing a child. Most bosses are not this cruel, but even this behavior was acceptable for the company's top management, and no one would criticize him. His subordinates could not speak against their superior, and his colleagues did not say anything; they did not want to harm their relationship with him.

Changing jobs at the age of twenty-four is difficult for anyone, but especially for a woman. Many companies prefer to hire younger women; older women without fiancés are less likely to marry and to leave. A woman who changes her job is sometimes looked upon with suspicion. Personnel officers wonder whether she had to quit her previous job because she had problems getting along with her bosses, problems that could carry over into her next job.

Since leaving Brother, Hitomi has taken on several part-time jobs. She teaches her cousins English and spends her days at home doing chores for her family. She lives with an older brother, who is a salaryman, and two younger sisters, who are OLs. Her parents run a mom-and-pop store in Utsumi, selling clothes that her mother sews or her father buys from wholesalers. Hitomi told me, ''I get up every morning at 6:00. I make myself a cup of coffee and start the laundry. I make breakfast and have it ready on the kitchen table by 7:00 when the rest of the family wakes up. I read the newspaper and watch television after I finish washing the dishes. Then, I clean the bathrooms, air out the futons, and tidy up the living room. I make lunch for my parents and watch soap operas on TV. At 6:00 P.M., I make dinner and eat with my parents.''

Hitomi says that her days are full and that she enjoys living at home, although her parents keep asking her when she will marry. She realizes that she will only be marriageable for a couple more years. She knows that an OL's life is difficult but continues to search the classified ads for clerical jobs in companies. As an OL, Hitomi will make more money, encounter people outside of her local community, and perhaps meet the man she will marry.

An Ping

An Ping was the only non-Japanese OL the company had ever hired. A resident of Taiwan until she was twenty, she moved with her family to Japan when her sister married a Japanese salaryman. An Ping went to a university in Kyushu to study English literature. She enjoyed university life; in the foreign students' program, she made friends with students from France, Germany, the United States, Tanzania—places she had read about but never visited.

After graduating from college, An Ping looked for a job where she would be able to use her English, Chinese, and Japanese language abilities. Many of her college classmates found jobs as English teachers in Japanese companies. An Ping scanned the want ads for positions in companies, applied to several, and was accepted by four. She settled on Brother because the salary was "fair," and because she was told that she would be able to use her Chinese and English abilities. She thought that Brother, unlike other companies that she interviewed with, put women to "practical use."

An Ping moved into the company women's dormitory and became an OL in the industrial sewing machine division, even though she felt that she would be more useful in the overseas divisions of the sales company. Her requests to transfer to sales were ignored. She commented: "Kobayashi-san and others in the personnel division presented my case to the directors, but they wouldn't hear of it. They had never had any non-Japanese Asian OLs in that company. I don't understand why they prefer to struggle with OLs and salarymen without the proper English or Chinese ability than take me on."

Her dreams of being put to "practical use" at the company were shattered. An Ping left the company in 1987 to marry a well-paid Japanese salaryman in the Toyota Motor Company, which had decided to transfer him to its Taiwan subsidiary for two years. She married him—as she puts it—not for love but because "she was getting old" and "wanted to live in Taiwan." She felt that she would grow to love him. An Ping and her husband have moved to Taiwan.

Living in Japan and working full-time in a Japanese company, An Ping was subject to the same pressures as Japanese women. She abandoned her dreams of having a challenging job where her skills would be put to good use. Disillusioned, she left the company in a manner that met social expectations: she got married and contributed to the turnover of the company's women workers.

In this chapter, I have described the lives of individual factory women who, for the most part, come from lower-income families and suffer the hardships of laboring on a factory assembly line, and of office ladies who are better off financially but also face problems with bosses and leave the company. The company has no place for women who hang on, or try to offer their own opinions. This disturbs the harmony of the workplace, a balance built strictly upon well-defined male and female roles.

Women's lives at the company are much more diverse than I have shown. There are many exceptions: the factory women whose fathers are company presidents, for example, and office ladies who receive special treatment because they are related to the top managers of the company. But these cases are rare. In the introduction to *Working*, Studs Terkel explains that all workers have certain gripes about their work. Factory workers have the "blue collar blues," and office workers have the "white collar moans." I have tried to bring some of the blues and moans and self-perceptions of Japanese women to light.

CHAPTER SIX

Acceptance and Understanding

MY COMPANY INTERNSHIP ended in September 1987. I had seen many things and experienced much. I returned to school to ponder how the company structure affected Japanese women's views of their world. I looked back at the lives of factory women and office ladies in Nagoya and attempted to give an accurate account of how they are controlled by and in conflict with the company.

I had gathered information on how women viewed their lives in the company using three different approaches—a questionnaire, interviews, and fieldwork. With the questionnaires and the interviews, I tried to understand these women as an outsider looking in. By participating in their society, I gained a different vantage point, that of an inside observer. As an "insider," I do not mean to imply that I was considered to be a Japanese OL, factory woman, or dormitory resident. Anthropologists describe the concept of the Japanese group and a distinctive inside-outside dichotomy (Nakane 1970; T. S. Lebra 1976). In my case, I felt that my entry into the lives and society of the Japanese progressed in degrees. I started as a complete outsider and made slow and difficult steps toward the "inside."

When I first arrived in Nagoya, I had the problem of acceptance. I was shown great hospitality by my office group. My bosses threw welcoming parties in my honor. I was served tea and treated differently from other women in the office; this kept me on the outside.

Acceptance varies with the context of the fieldwork. Different subjects will react in many different ways toward the researcher. I found it necessary to adapt to the rules that my subjects lived by. This was the most difficult aspect of my work. As a factory woman, I had to work long hours on an assembly line. When I was an OL, I deferred to the bosses. And I observed the rules of Aoi dormitory when I lived there. Initial acceptance of the rules of each context made assimilation easier.

I found that there were many different levels of acceptance. My work group treated me extraordinarily well because of the illustrious connection with which I had entered the company—Professor Ezra Vogel of Harvard University, well-known throughout Japan for his book *Japan as Number One*. They associated me with Professor Vogel and with Harvard, a school that they believed graduated the "best and brightest" of the United States. They treated me like a VIP, which worked to my disadvantage.

Yet I was also Asian in heritage and features. I was told, six months after I started working in the office, "When I saw you for the first time, I was very surprised. I asked myself, 'Is she really American?'" Many of my coworkers "forgot" that I was as American as someone who had blond hair and blue eyes. My appearance was not a constant reminder of our cultural differences. Informants expected me to have a good understanding of Asian family values and of women's roles in society.

Some of the women in my dormitory and at work were eager informants who readily gave their opinions and thoughts about Japanese society. Unlike most Japanese women, who were shy and somewhat hesitant to approach foreigners, these women wanted to be seen with foreigners, who they thought were exotic. They felt this would improve their image among the Japanese. It was the women whom I met later in the year, through much effort, who gave mainstream opinions.

Slowly and through perseverance, I made friends in the dormitory. I befriended the women who lived in the room next to mine by visiting them every night, bringing them cake, crackers, or chocolate. The first day, they asked me the questions that are commonly asked of young female foreigners: "How do you like Japan? Who are your favorite pop singers? Do you have a boyfriend?" I taught myself how to knit so that I could join them in late-night talking and knitting sessions.

After two weeks of knitting, they no longer asked questions. They did not treat me like a visitor, and I no longer brought food to their room. After a month, they began to tell me things about themselves; they told me about their boyfriends and showed me photos of their families. They had been apprehensive and secretive about their personal lives before. I felt close to them when we joked in the bath, or play wrestled in the lobby and fell down laughing in fits of giggles. After they married and left the company, I visited their homes to continue our eating and television-watching sessions. We were very different but shared many common interests and sensitivities. They accepted me as their foreign friend, despite the differences in views of life courses, marriage, and women's roles.

Getting close to the OLs in the office was more difficult. When I first arrived, I was very Western in dress and mannerisms. I finally bought Nagoya clothes and traded in my flats for high heels. I also assumed affectations of innocence and engaged in normal OL conversations. I gained a small degree of acceptance from some of the eighteen- and nineteen-year-old OLs, who gave me Donald Duck paraphernalia and held my hand as I walked about the office. After about two months, the rest of the OLs began to invite me to discos with them, and into their homes.

I got mixed reactions from my bosses. Some treated me as if I were an OL, gave me orders, and asked me to serve tea. Others continued to be formal and polite. After three months, I had found a niche in the workplace. Being a foreigner became less of an issue.

When my first internship at Brother ended in February 1987, I had gained many friendships, but I still felt that I received more attention than the other OLs.

When I returned to the office as an OL in August 1987 my reception was different. No parties were thrown. People treated me like an employee who had come back from a long business trip. The people were the same, but the tone of the workplace had become more serious. The bosses were giving women extra responsibilities. In light of the damaging appreciation of the yen, OLs and salarymen had dropped the formalities and went about their work. They expected me to do my best, too. Things became more egalitarian for me, and bosses and salarymen had no qualms about yelling at me for mistakes. The first time I worked in the office I had translated manuals, but this time I was given more responsibility: I wrote product evaluations in Japanese and worked on a direct sales program. When I went out with OLs, I felt that I was more of a participant in their conversations, and less of an observer.

After I returned to Harvard, a salaryman from my section came to Cambridge on a business trip and visited me. Exchanging Japan-America notes, he confided that I had been treated like a stranger the first time I worked in the office. But the second time, everyone knew me and treated me like a regular employee. I thus had gained another level of acceptance.

In the factory, the road to acceptance was a rocky one. I met violent opposition from some women, made instant friendships with others, and elicited apathy from most. The factory was short-handed and took in many part-timers. New faces appeared on the line every day. Some factory women disliked me because I came from Harvard, and they made envious comments like: "You have so many opportunities. American women are so lucky." One woman went as far as to take apart my work, redo it, and tell me that I "couldn't do anything right." This slowed down the line until one of the senior workers came by and assured her that I was doing a good job. In time, I could make friends with most of the other women.

Conclusion

In the introduction to this book, I asked the question, "How do Brother women view their working lives?" My fieldwork, interviews, and questionnaires indicate that women see work as a prelude to marriage and raising children, not as an objective in itself. This view is reflected in the paternalistic company rules and in the domestic roles assigned to women in the workplace. Women are discouraged from pursuing careers at Brother; they do not expect to be promoted, and they are under social pressure to follow the conventions to marry, quit their job, and devote their energies to the family. Office ladies who do not conform to these social expectations become objects of gossip and pity.

OLs experience more pressures from the *shigarami* social network of company relationships than do their sisters in the factory. The OLs, who have much more contact with others in their work group, are careful not to damage relationships with coworkers. Factory women, who are less conscious of group relationships, leave the company because the work is physically and psychologically draining and unpleasant—not because they feel that they are getting too old, and others expect them to leave. The factory women who stay for ten or fifteen years seem to be the most disconsolate. They may have suffered great personal losses or realized that they will never marry and have no other means to support themselves besides factory work. Women marry at younger ages to escape this fate. The turnover of female laborers ensures the company a constant pool of fresh young workers who are paid the low wages of employees without seniority.

Brother employment statistics (see appendix) show a substantial annual turnover of women workers. Company women typically work from the time they finish school until they marry or have children, while men in the company work until they retire at fifty-five or sixty-five. Labor-force participation statistics for Japan in 1985 show a similar phenomenon (figure 3).

Figure 3. **Labor Force Participation by Sex, 1985**

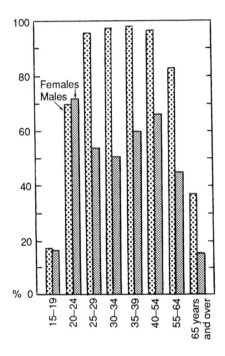

Source: The Statistical Handbook of Japan, 1986, p. 106.

To summarize, as members of the workplace, OLs must conform to the expected behavior of company women and carry out ''domestic'' responsibilities: they serve tea to their superiors (the men in the office), keep themselves presentable and feminine, and do the cleaning. The source of male authority lies in the hierarchical structure of the work group. The OLs' consciousness of the fragility of the *shigarami* network of relationships forces them to accept their status with magnanimity. OLs work toward preserving relationships and upholding group expectations, the final one of which is that they will quit their job and marry before they reach thirty. Those who do not conform ''lose face'' and find themselves unwanted.

In chapter two, I described the labor conditions in the Mizuho factory. Simone Weil, the French philosopher, once described assembly-line work as "work that laborers could not sympathize with" (1977, 63). They rarely get the satisfaction of seeing the finished product. Women say that they "grease, fasten screws, attach wires," but seldom do they say that they "build typewriters." Women work under harsh conditions for long hours, with overtime demands and occasional harrassment by bosses. They internalize their disappointment and ungrudgingly serve the ends of the company. Many shrug, "The company is being selfish again" and give up their precious weekends and "after-six" time to work on the line.

The factory, however, is more democratic than the office in the treatment of women. Women look up to female senior workers who guide and instruct them. They have limited contact with men and never have to serve tea. Women are allowed to stay on until retirement age and can advance to the level of senior worker if they gain seniority or, more importantly, demonstrate leadership abilities. The company is less concerned with the turnover of factory women than of OLs. Most factory women enter the company after junior high or high school, and their wages remain low in spite of their seniority. They tend to quit their jobs anyway, not because of perceived pressure from the company but because of the nature of factory work, which most women find exhausting. They work to pay for their dowries and quit as soon as they find a husband. Marriage is the ticket out of suffering and hard work. Those who do not marry become the casualties of the system and are doomed to remain in a Japanese company that makes few provisions for senior women workers.

In chapter four, I examined the company dormitory life and its relationship to the turnover process of female labor. The dormitory is just one of the company's *in loco parentis* structures—a home away from home for many of the women employees who live too far away to commute to work. Women receive housing, meals, and a bath, but they are expected to act like "obedient company daughters,'' do housekeeping, and observe strict rules on curfews, morality, and general tidiness. The purpose of the dormitory is twofold. First, it protects the women from the defiling influences of the outside world. The parents of Aoi dormitory residents can rest assured that their daughters remain safe, well cared for, and chaste, under the watchful eyes of the dormitory supervisor. Second, the dormitory system perpetuates the turnover of female labor. Women who live at the dormitory are expected to marry and to leave the company. Residents take classes in bridal skills and often talk about marriage. They are crowded into small rooms with incompatible roommates and are restricted in their daily lives. As a result, many look to marriage as a way out of the dormitory and work.

The Future

In light of the damaging effects of trade friction, the appreciation of the yen, and the labor shortage in Japan, Brother is beginning to expect more and more of its OL labor force. These women still do clerical work, but the volume of work has increased. The director of the personnel division stated in 1987, ''Men in the company will do about sixty hours of overtime a month, and women, about twenty.'' These estimates were modest. That year, company OLs were no longer required to take lessons in serving tea during their first week of training. (They still serve tea, but the classes are gone.)

At a 1986 meeting of company's policy makers and local academics to discuss the equal employment law, the director of the personnel division acknowledged that in the present age of ''women's action . . . we can no longer say that the women won't work, that they will quit the company soon after they are hired, or that women have no ability. Maybe we should look at things from a woman's perspective.'' He added, ''Women don't always have the same abilities as men, but sometimes there are women who do. Maybe we should manage them as if they were men.'' Things are changing at Brother and in many other Japanese firms, but at a snail's pace. The personnel department recognizes that women have the potential to be good workers yet continues to bar them from management positions.

A woman's view of the world helps to determine her relationships and position in society. Female workers at Brother have a black-and-white world view. In my questionnaire, I gave company women a list of duties and asked them to state who was responsible for them—women or men. Ninety-two percent said that men are responsible for making money. The other 8 percent said that this duty should be shared by both men and women. Over 90 percent answered that management of the household, shopping, cleaning, and food preparation are solely female responsibilities.

Many of the women at Brother expressed that their life and work choices are limited by the social expectation of marriage. Ironically, most also seem to aspire to ''lives of domesticity.'' I wonder if these perceptions will change as women begin to take on more responsible roles in the workplace. Further research into women's perceptions of roles and of marriage will provide a greater understanding of women's views on work.

Now, as the Japanese economy continues to expand, and as the labor shortage becomes more acute, a few Japanese firms are starting to take notice of the great stores of talent they have right in their own company—their female employees. Many are following the lead of the growing number of foreign firms that have come to Japan to do business, which offer positions of responsibility to women.

These Japanese firms ask women at the initial recruitment stage whether they would like to do *ippanshoku* (work that OLs do) or enter the *sogoshoku* (management) track and do the same work that men do. The women who choose the *sogoshoku* track work under the same conditions as the men. They are not expected to serve tea, and they often work in the office until 8:00 or 9:00 every night.

The *sogoshoku* women, however, represent the elite of the

female work force. Most are university-educated and fluent in one or more foreign languages. And most companies, including Brother, do not offer women *sogoshoku* responsibilities, maintaining that they can be handled only by men.

Because of the lack of adequate childcare facilities, most women in the management track are forced to retire when they have children. A woman is only allowed to work if she can juggle her work responsibilities with those at home.

The increasing presence of women in the management track marks a change in female employment. Nevertheless, improvements in the lives and conditions of working women on the whole will come slowly, and many of Japan's OLs and factory women can expect little change in their current conditions.

Questionnaire and Results

I JOINED the Life Research Center section, the academic center of Brother, in the fall of 1986. Composed of graduates of the most prestigious colleges in Japan (University of Tokyo, Kyoto University, Nara Women's College, and others), the LRC did important market research upon which the management based their corporate decisions. This group conducted questionnaires and interviews on topics of interest to the company. It was vaguely interested in analyzing the work consciousness of contemporary working women in Japan. This project was of secondary importance to the success of the company so it was placed on the proverbial back burner, and LRC members were reluctant to commit themselves to it. I spoke to one of the supervisors about my interest in Japanese women's issues. Following our conversation, the LRC asked me to join the group and to take on this project.

Three LRC women—Matsui, Nakamura, and Aizawa—helped me with this project. The LRC management assigned these female advisers to me because they felt that women would better understand issues concerning other women. Both men and women in the company believed that their worlds were distinct. The LRC, like others at the company, believed that each sex had specific life roles and understandings that were not shared or comprehended by the opposite sex. Furthermore, it was expected that women would take on research projects that were less important to the company than the men's assignments. LRC women did market research on minor products, polled customer opinions, provided tea service, and cleaned the office. The men were busy with more important work: market research on typewriters, printers, sewing machines, and word processors—products that would determine the company's future success.

In researching this topic, we were first hindered by the paucity of literature on contemporary women workers in Japan. The few research papers and white papers that I found based their analyses on questionnaire research alone; they gave little consideration to the individuals involved or to possible inconsistencies. Statistical data not supplemented with interviews or personal sources told me little about the lives of women who worked in the factories or offices.

The LRC highly recommended Professor Yoshida's *The Consciousness and Life of Contemporary Women*, a scholarly work on Japanese women, but I found that it used the same techniques as other publications. The research center wanted me to model my analysis after the work of Professor Reiko Sekiguchi, a sociologist at the Seitoku Gakuen. In "Life Cycles and the Way Women Live," a chapter in Yoshida's book, Sekiguchi uses statistical information to divide the life of a Japanese woman into four stages. The first stage is growth and education, which ends when the young woman leaves the home she grew up in. "The most basic household has two children. In such a family, the average age of marriage for the husband is 26.9 and for the wife is 23.8. The second child is born 2.4 years after the first" (p. 34). Sekiguchi notes that the third stage of a woman's life begins when her children leave home, and the fourth stage begins when her husband retires, typically at age sixty-five. Average ages for death are 70.2 for men and 75.6 for women.

Sekiguchi's analysis, based on statistical data, provides a good description of the averages. But it does not discuss what kinds of women—blue collar or white collar—best represent this kind of life course, or who the exceptions are. This analysis suggests, for example, that most women will gain independence from their families and children at specific ages, but it does not tell us who these women are, why they make these life choices, or anything about the society in which they live. Sekiguchi's model helps us to understand women broadly but does not tell us anything about how the society in which these women live affects their life choices.

Making models from statistical data without analysis is an accepted methodology in Japan. Studies conducted by insurance companies, social scientists, and government analysts depend heavily on questionnaire results. I believed that the questionnaire results could be supplemented by information from fieldwork and interviews to give a better understanding of women's lives in the company.

As I took notes on life in the company and set up interviews, the LRC and I set out to make a questionnaire. We started with an unconventional approach. We read through what were labeled as "soft touch" magazines—*More, An An, 25ans,* the women's publications in Japan that are filled with articles on marriage and women's consciousness. These magazines frequently publish reader questionnaires on women's concerns. The questions point out many different types of things that female readers are interested in, but many of the stories are implausible. The articles present larger-than-life female sophisticates with glamorous lifestyles, sports cars, and starry-eyed fiancés. Nowhere in the pages could I find anyone resembling a Nagoya assembly line worker or an office lady in an old-fashioned blue uniform serving tea to her boss. We also read the few insurance company surveys that we found in the library, but we could not find any academic papers on factory women or OLs.

Two OLs in the advertising division warned: " 'Soft touch' isn't real. The articles are all about career women in Tokyo or women in the katakana professions. 'Soft touch' shows our dreams, but there are many things that these magazines do not show us, like the long, hard days that OLs have to work, or the less-than-glamorous lives that they return to after work. Working women have to make sacrifices for their families and work for temperamental bosses for little pay. This is the reality for the women, not the shining images of the designers, stewardesses, or women in management.''

We made a master list of the types of questions used in other surveys, and based other questions on my own experiences as a participant observer in the company. Many of the questions about marriage and work were inspired by daily office and factory conversations. I wanted to write a questionnaire that the respondents themselves could relate to.

The Questionnaire Sample

The company employs five thousand workers in its offices and factories in Nagoya; approximately two thousand are female. The personnel division asked me to limit the number of women in the sample to two hundred. Therefore, I decided to focus on a specific group: the unmarried women who had joined the company in the previous four years (1983–1986). Limiting my sample made it easier to analyze the results. It would have been difficult to compare the answers given by an unmarried, twenty-year-old OL to those of a married, fifty-year-old part-time factory woman. The group I focused on excluded all of the older factory women who had decided never to marry, as well as the married women who worked in the factories to support their families.

We selected the subjects after examining the company's female employment records, provided by the personnel division. We looked at figures on the women hired and remaining in Brother, their educational records, and their work assignments. The personnel division could only give us statistics but could provide no personal information (such as an individual's educational background, her reasons for joining or leaving the company, her family background), as that would have violated the company's agreement to keep such information confidential. Tables A-1 and A-2 give statistics on the total female work force.

Looking at only the entries of women hired from 1983 to 1986,

Table A–1

Women Employed at Brother, 1983–1986, by Workplace

	Factory	Office	Total
1983	131	84	215
1984	93	122	215
1985	99	155	254
1986	99	153	252
Total	422	514	936

Note: Some of the women who work in the factories may be OLs, designers, or data processors.

Table A–2

Women Workers by Educational Level

	1977	1978	1979	1980	1981	1982	1983	1984	1985	1986
Graduates of four-year colleges										
No. employed[a]	5	3	0	5	15	21	24	35	50	38
No. remaining[b]	0	0	0	1	5	14	15	21	48	38
Graduates of junior colleges										
No. employed	5	6	0	7	10	22	18	37	65	78
No. remaining	0	1	0	4	7	15	13	34	65	75
High school graduates										
No. employed	282	104	6	59	170	282	173	145	139	137
No. remaining	21	16	3	27	83	160	111	128	138	136

[a]Women hired by the company during the specified year.
[b]Women from the specified year who were still employed at Brother at the time of the study, on December 12, 1986.

we created a table of 200 questionnaire subjects (table A-3). The breakdown (by education) of this sample group was roughly proportional to the actual educational levels of the company women hired in 1983–1986.

Table A–3

Questionnaire Subjects, by Education Level

	1983	1984	1985	1986	Total
College	6	9	19	16	50
Jr. college	4	9	17	20	50
High school	21	25	27	27	100

The personnel division did not have the exact figures of factory women and OLs in the company. They knew the workplaces that the women had been assigned to, but not their actual work content. We did not know whether the factory women were doing clerical or on-line factory work, although we knew that the majority of them were line workers, not OLs. We knew that these women were in their twenties.

Members of the LRC picked random office and factory sections throughout the company. We based the number of questionnaires sent to each workplace on the table of 200 subjects (table A-3). After the questionnaires were printed, we sent them to different sections in the company that we knew were composed mainly or entirely of high school, junior high school, or college graduates. Uncertain of the type of responses that we might get, we used all 224 questionnaires that had been printed, randomly distributing the extra 24 into packets. We asked the section chiefs to give the questionnaires to women who had been hired between 1983 and 1986.

Response

Within three days, 218 of the original 224 questionnaires had been returned by company mail. We were surprised by the overwhelming response, which had not been mandatory.

I received much support for my research from the women. Many expressed interest in knowing how other women responded to the questionnaire. A woman in the dormitory said, "This is the first time that anyone—other than my family or friends—has asked for my opinions on work and marriage."

Within their social groups, company women often discussed marriage, work, daily concerns, and their futures, but rarely on a questionnaire. I believe that two things in particular intrigued them—that it was the first time that anyone had attempted to examine their lives, and that the person conducting the study was foreign.

Even the male directors of the company were interested: they asked me to present my results to them and explain how the "life consciousness" of women in the United States compares with that of women in Japan.

Results

When the questionnaires were returned, we entered the results into the computer and used the SASSP statistical analysis program to summarize the raw data for each item.

The questionnaire was composed of three parts—sections on work, marriage, and family/self background. In the work section, I asked questions about work ambitions, reasons for choosing the company, reasons for working, types of work done, and satisfaction or dissatisfaction with the company. In the marriage section, I asked women about their hopes for marriage and marriage partners and their perceived roles; and in the last section, I asked general questions on education, leisure, and family. For the purposes of this discussion, I will limit the results discussed to those that relate to the role of the company in the lives of the women.

The answers varied widely. First, I looked at the answers to questions on the third section. I had intended to eliminate any discrepancy by polling only the single women who were hired in the previous four years. But other differences remained, especially

Figure A-1. **Age Distribution of Respondents**

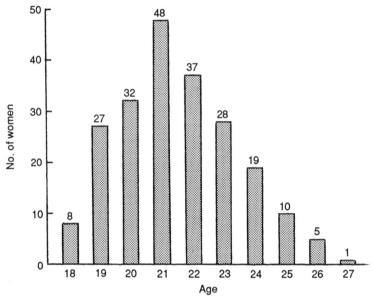

Note: Three did not respond to this question.

those between the women who came from low-income families and the women who came from middle- or upper-class families. There were regional differences that could not be accounted for in the original sample. Some women came from cities; others from rural areas. Although I was assured that the women polled were under thirty years of age, there are, of course, worlds of difference between a woman in her early twenties and one who is twenty-nine. I attempt to account for these differences and to explain certain answers in the following discussion of the questionnaire results.

Graphing the women's ages showed me that there was a great tendency to leave the company after working for several years (figure A-1). Three of the women surveyed left this answer blank.

The ages of the women in the sample range from eighteen to twenty-seven. Most high school graduates enter the company at age

Figure A-2. **Distribution of Respondents by Year Hired**

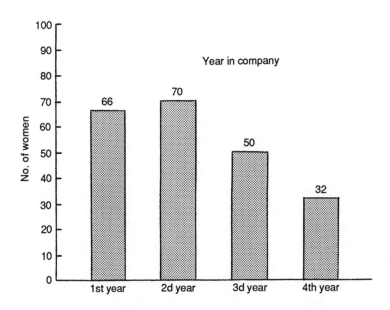

eighteen or nineteen, and junior college women enter at twenty. This accounts for a steady increase in the number of female workers from ages eighteen to twenty-one. At twenty there is a significant drop in the number of women workers. One would expect an increase here since most college graduates join the company at this time. This drop shows that many high school graduates leave the company before age twenty-two. Brother employs few twenty-four-year-olds.

Could the number of twenty-one-year-old respondents be due to an overrepresentation of high school graduates in their third year? Examination of the years in which respondents entered the company and their educational levels shows that this is not the case (figure A-2 and table A-4).

Women of all four years were represented in almost equal proportion to the actual number of women in the company.

Table A–4

Year of Entry into the Company

	1983	1984	1985	1986
All women workers	139	183	251	249
Percentage	16.9	22.3	30.5	30.3
Respondents	33	50	70	66
Percentage	15.1	22.9	32.1	30.2

Among respondents, high school graduates are under-represented while college graduates are overrepresented (figure A-3 and table A-5). This must be kept in mind when looking at the rest of the data.

Answers to the question "What kind of work do you do?" (figure A-4) underlined the difficulty of making distinctions between OLs and factory women. We pondered in which category we should place the women who program and keypunch, those who do technical work in the factories but do not assemble machines, and those who design the exteriors of sewing machines and home appliances.

Table A–5

Last School Attended

	College	Jr. college	High school
All women workers	122	187	513
Percentage	14.8	22.8	62.4
Respondents[a]	56	48	112
Percentage	25.7	22.0	43.1

[a]Two women did not answer this question. The women who answered "vocational school" were placed in the high school category, as were those who answered "other." Most women went to high school. Vocational schools are attended by high-school-age students.

Figure A-3. **Distribution of Respondents by Educational Level**

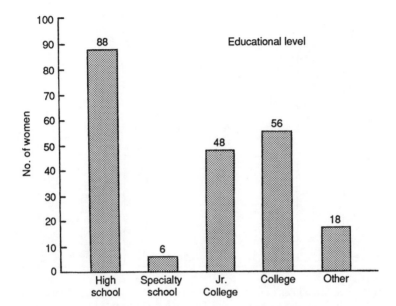

Note: Two did not respond to this question.

Members of the LRC suggested that I group the respondents into four categories: the women who worked in offices or did planning and research work became OLs; those who assembled parts or tested equipment on the line were factory women; female programmers and keypunchers were placed into the engineer category; and the designers had their own grouping. Two women did not answer this question.

The following questions relate to the women's life choices. The first question in the section on work asked, ''Why do you work?'' The answers are graphed in figure A-5.

The respondents wrote their top two of nine choices. The top six responses for first and second choices are given in table A-6.

The answers depend greatly on individual lifestyles. Women who live in their own apartments or in the dormitory will work to

Figure A-4. **Distribution of Respondents by Type of Work**

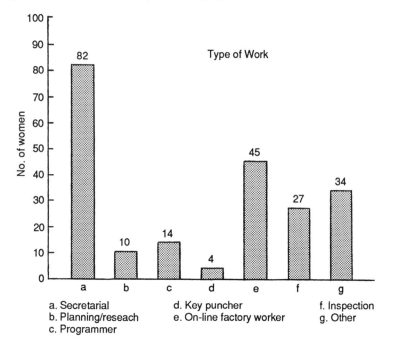

a. Secretarial   d. Key puncher   f. Inspection
b. Planning/reseach   e. On-line factory worker g. Other
c. Programmer

Note: Two did not respond to this question.

pay for their living expenses—rent, food, etc. Tazuko, a factory woman in the dormitory, noted: "After I pay for my room and board, gifts, clothes, and other things, I have very little money left. Some of it goes into savings, the rest for leisure. I think about marriage but I can't save for it. I think that my parents will pay for that." Women who live at home, on the other hand, have few living expenses. They are dependent on their parents and are more likely to save for marriage or spend money on leisure. Yet some face daily pressures from their parents to find a husband. Junko, a twenty-four-year-old OL, commented: "My parents are so annoying. They're always trying to set me up with dates, and asking me if I am saving enough money for my dowry." Women who live in the dormitory have less pressure

Figure A-5. **Why Women Work**

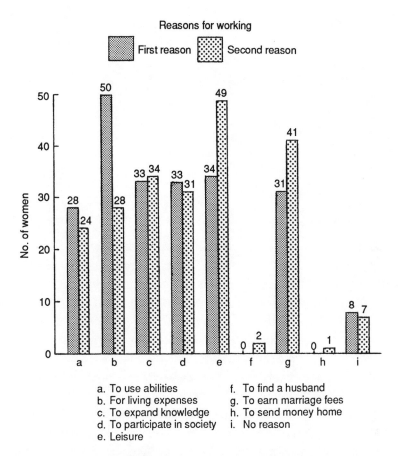

from their parents to marry. They are nudged into marriage by other means: they marry because they do not enjoy their work, or because they do not like living in the dormitory. Twenty of the thirty-one women who answered that they worked to save money for marriage were factory women; the rest were junior college graduates. There were no college graduates.

It is difficult to place significance measures on the "first choice" and "second choice" answers to this question. A woman could

Table A–6

Top Two Reasons for Working

	No. of respondents	Percentage
First choice		
To cover living expenses	50	22.9
To pay for leisure	34	15.6
To increase knowledge	33	15.1
To participate in society	33	15.1
To save for marriage	31	14.2
To use my skills	28	12.8
Second choice		
To pay for leisure	49	22.5
Marriage	41	18.8
To increase knowledge	34	15.6
To participate in society	31	14.2
To cover living expenses	28	12.8
To use my skills	24	11.0

work for more than two reasons. The answers do not reveal all of the respondents' work intentions, but they do highlight the most popular reasons that women have for working, and other answers that women avoided. For example, few women said that they worked ''to use (their) skills,'' suggesting that perhaps they were not interested in pursuing careers. Only two women said that they came to the company to find a husband, and one said that she worked to send money home to her parents.

I asked women how long they intended to work in the company (figure A-6). Sixty-five (29.8 percent) said that they will work until they have children but wanted to work again when the children grew up. Sixty-four (29.4 percent) wanted to work only until they married. Thirty-three (15.1 percent) said they wanted to stop working when they had children and never work again. Thirty-nine (17.9 percent) wanted to keep working even if they married and had children. Fifteen wanted to quit at their first possible chance.

These answers suggest two dominant trends of thinking about life choices. Most women prefer either marriage or work. The women who prefer marriage look upon it as a means of escape from

Figure A-6. **How Long Women Work**

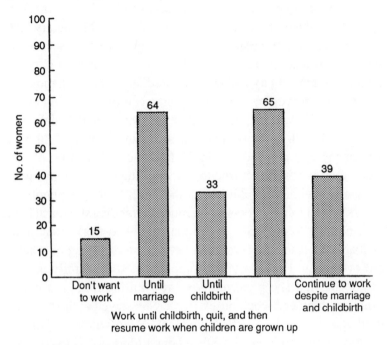

Note: Two did not respond to this question.

their working lives in the offices or factories. They want to leave the company at their first possible chance—when they marry. Women who do not mind working plan to quit their jobs when they have a child—they believe that it is impossible to juggle work with their responsibilities as mothers—and find another job when their children are grown up and no longer need to be looked after.

Many of the first-year female workers who preferred marriage over work became engaged at their first possible chance and left the company within months. One such woman, who lived on my floor in the dormitory, told me during one of our late-night sweater-knitting, tea-drinking sessions, "What I'd really like to do is live in a house, and be a housewife. That way, I can do all of the things that I enjoy. I only have to get up early in the morning to make breakfast for my husband. After he leaves for work, I am free to do whatever I like until he comes home for dinner." In January 1987, she announced her engagement to an engineer in her section. By April of the next year, she was a housewife in Inazawa City. Her dreams of domesticity had been realized, and she was happy.

Other women enjoy work and want to continue working as long as possible. They think that being a housewife is dull. Chiaki is the only married OL in the Brother Sales downtown office. Miho was one of the few married OLs in Brother Industries. Both of them enjoy their work and refused to quit after they married men in the company. Neither has children. Miho said, "I like the people that I work with. I think work is really much better than staying at home with nothing to do." She added that she liked work because her husband did it too. It gave her a better understanding of what he did every day. Her salary also supplemented the family income. Miho said that she preferred work to "killing time in a culture center with other bored housewives." She stayed at the company until she was eight months' pregnant. Miho enjoyed work and wants to return to it one day when her children go off to college.

I asked women what they felt was more important, personal life or work (figure A-7). A total of 192 (88 percent) said that they valued personal life over work. In an informal poll, I asked some salarymen in the sales company the same question. Unhesitatingly, they all replied that work was more important than personal life. Of course, the men's answers reflect certain values in the Japanese company. Men who say that they value personal life over their working lives at the company are looked upon with suspicion.

There were rare exceptions, however. One section chief in Brother Industries was infamous for giving the appearance that he valued personal life over work. Kato came to work at 8:00 every morning, worked until 5:00 P.M., and occasionally took breaks, standing by his desk and practicing his golf swing. At precisely 5:00 he left the office. He placed his desk by the window and was

Figure A-7. **Relative Importance of Personal Life versus Work**

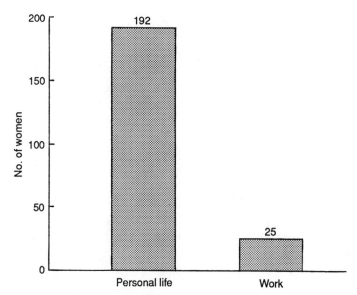

Note: One did not respond to this question.

called "the employee who gazes dreamily out of the window and ignores his work" by his subordinates, who took careful note of his behavior. They said things like: "Kato is so noisy. He's always talking. I can't get any work done when he's here." "He always leaves at 5:00. I work until 9:00 or 10:00 every night." "Kato is really eccentric. I think that he stares out of the window every day." Kato's behavior was looked upon with scorn. He has since left the company.

Women, however, are expected to leave work at 6:00 P.M. When I explained the questionnaire results to the company directors, they took the responses to mean that women care less about their work than men do. Perhaps a more accurate interpretation would be that women value personal life over work because they have no interest in the menial tasks they have been assigned.

Figure A-8. **Satisfaction with Work and Workplace**

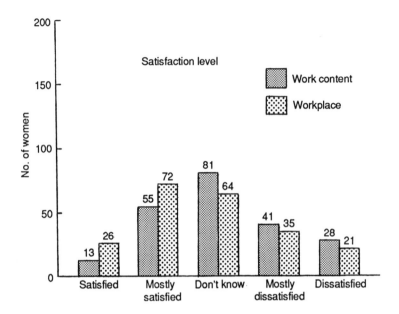

Polling the women on their satisfaction in the workplace revealed that the majority of the women liked their workplace to some degree, but most did not care for the actual content of their jobs (figure A-8).

I wondered if the women would prefer to do the jobs that men did. Figure A-9 shows the responses to the question, ''Do you want to do a job with the same level of responsibility as a man in the company?'' Most women said that they did. Fifty-one stated that they were sure that they did, while 104 said that they would like to if it were something that they could handle.

Women realize, of course, that doing a man's job does not guarantee entry into a salaryman's world. The after-hours business that salarymen conduct in hostess bars with clients over beer, whiskey, and sake would still be off-limits for a woman. Men and women would remain cognizant of their differences when they met

Figure A-9. **Opinions on Having the Same Work Responsibilities as Men**

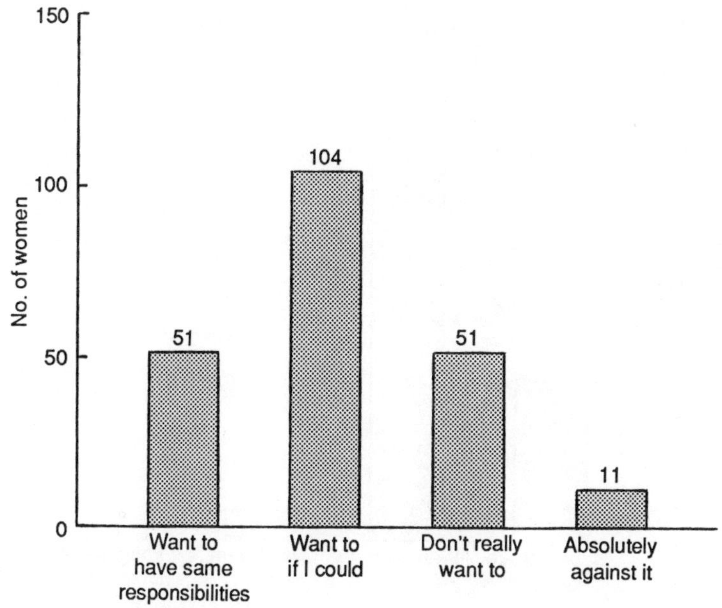

Note: One did not respond to this question.

in a social setting. The woman would still have to serve tea and clean the office, while her salarymen "equals" would not. And she would be expected to quit her job when she has children. It is extremely difficult for a woman to hold down a responsible job and raise children. She would be expected to work long hours in the office, or at least to stay late in the office to show her commitment to her work group. As a mother, she would be responsible for single-handedly raising the children and seeing that they were well-educated. Men, on the other hand, work in the company until late, come home to a meal and bath that their wives have prepared for them, and see their children on the weekends. They are not responsible for raising the children, or for looking after them when they are sick, or for seeing that they get into the best schools in the nation.

Figure A-10. **Desire to Marry**

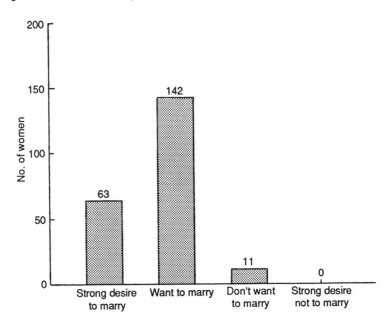

Note: Two did not respond to this question.

Only nineteen women (18.7 percent) said that they want a management position. When I worked in the company, there were no women in positions of management. Joining the management would be tantamount to entering a society devoid of women, where a woman would not be welcomed as an equal.

Responses to the section on marriage indicate that most women believe that marriage is a natural process in human life (figure A-10). Some 142 (65 percent) said that they wanted to marry; 63 (29 percent) expressed a ''strong desire'' to marry; 11 (5 percent) said that they wanted to remain single, but no one expressed a ''strong desire'' to remain single.

In the second part of the question, I asked at what age they wanted to marry (figure A-11). Of the 205 respondents who said they wanted to marry, 103 (50.2 percent) said they wanted to marry

Figure A-11. **Desired Age for Marriage**

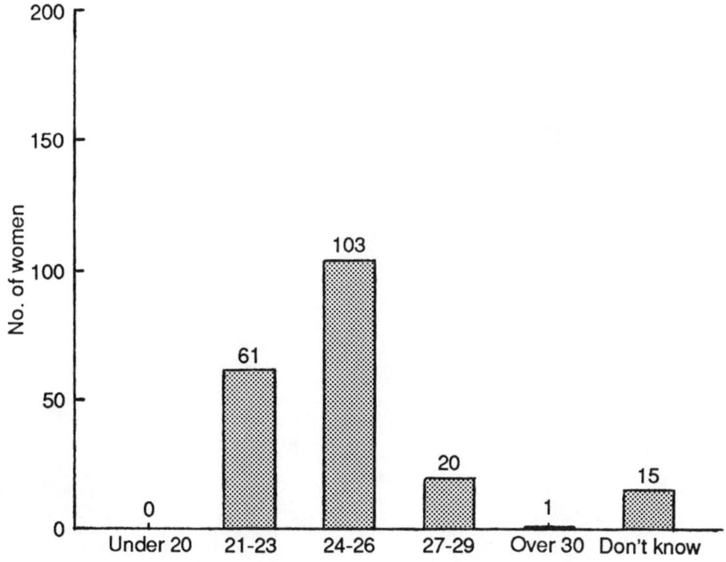

Note: Eighteen did not respond to this question.

between the ages of twenty-four and twenty-six. The second most popular choice was twenty-one to twenty-three years of age, chosen by 61 (29.8 percent) of the respondents.

I wondered if women felt they were fulfilling a social expectation by marrying. I asked why they wanted to marry (figure A-12). Women were asked to select the answers that applied. Eighty percent said that they wanted to marry so they "could live with someone they loved"; 62.4 percent wanted to marry for "psychological stability"; and 22.4 percent wanted "economic security." Apparently, 20 percent of the women did not care about love but married for other reasons—7.8 percent said they would marry because of "outside/parental pressures."

Respondents' answers revealed certain ways in which Brother

Figure A-12. **Reasons for Marriage**

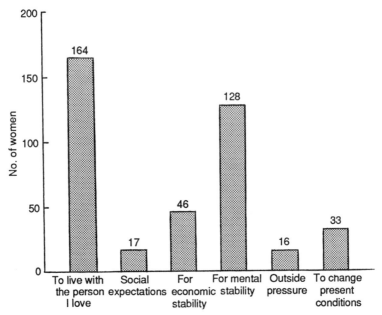

Note: Multiple responses allowed.

women workers view their lives. Marriage seems to be a natural, expected process for women. A significant number of women work to save money for marriage. Most will quit their jobs when they marry or have children. Many want to do work that men in the company do, but they do not want to enter a management-level position.

The questionnaire failed to explain how individual women viewed their lives in the company. What does an assembly-line woman, making typewriters, think about her work? Why does she feel this way? What does a woman mean when she says that she has a "strong desire" to marry? I could not begin to answer these questions until I supplemented my research with fieldwork and interviews. Questionnaires and other methodology complement each other: questionnaires show general trends, while interviews and fieldwork reveal individual and personal information.

From my interviews and my observations, I saw how many of the company women's life choices were affected by marriage and by conditions within the company. There are many other aspects of women's lives, such as recreation, home environment, views of bosses, and financial planning, that I did not consider. These deserve further study.

BIBLIOGRAPHY

Abegglen, James. *The Japanese Factory*. New York: Free Press, 1958.

Austin, Lewis, ed. *Japan: The Paradox of Progress*. New Haven: Yale University Press, 1969.

Befu, Harumi, and Edward Norbeck. "Japanese Usages of Terms of Relationship." *Southwestern Journal of Anthropology* 14 (1958): 66.

Bennett, John, and Ishino Iwao. *Paternalism in the Japanese Economy, Anthropological Studies of Oyabun-Kobun Patterns*. Minneapolis: University of Minnesota Press, 1963.

Bernstein, Gail. *Haruko's World*. Stanford: Stanford University Press, 1983.

Clark, Rodney. *The Japanese Company*. New Haven: Yale University Press, 1979.

Cole, Robert. *The Japanese Blue Collar*. Berkeley: University of California Press, 1970.

————. *Work, Mobility and Participation*. Berkeley: University of California Press, 1979.

Cook, Alice, and Hiroko Hayashi. *Working Women in Japan*. Ithaca: Cornell University Press, 1980.

Doi, Takeo. *The Anatomy of Dependence*. Tokyo: Kodansha, 1973.

————. "Giri-Ninjo: An Interpretation." In *Aspects of Social Change in Modern Japan*. Princeton: Princeton University Press, 1967.

Dore, Ronald P. *British Factory, Japanese Factory*. Berkeley: University of California Press, 1973.

———. "Mobility, Equality, and Individuation in Modern Japan." In *Aspects of Social Change in Modern Japan*. Princeton: Princeton University Press, 1967.

Eisler, Benita. *The Lowell Offering: Writings by New England Mill Women, 1840–1845*. Philadelphia: Lippincott, 1977.

Hane, Mikiso. *Peasants, Rebels and Outcasts*. New York: Pantheon Books, 1982.

Havens, Thomas. "Woman and War in Japan." *The American Historical Review* 80 (October 1975): 913.

Hendry, Joy. *Marriage in Changing Japan*. Tokyo: Charles Tuttle, 1981.

Kondo, Dorinne. "Gender, Self and Work in Japan; Some Issues in the Study of Self and Others." Ph.D. diss., Harvard University, 1982.

Koyama, Takashi. *The Changing Social Postion of Women in Japan*. New York: UNESCO, 1961.

Kung, Lydia. *Factory Women in Taiwan*. Cambridge: Cambridge University Press, 1981.

Lebra, Joyce, Joy Paulson, and Elizabeth Powers. *Women in Changing Japan*. Boulder: Westview Press, 1976.

Lebra, Takie Sugiyama. *Japanese Patterns of Behavior*. Honolulu: University of Hawaii Press, 1976.

———. *Japanese Women*. Honolulu: University of Hawaii Press, 1984.

Mannari, Hiroshi. *The Japanese Business Leaders*. Tokyo: University of Tokyo Press, 1974.

McCullough, William. "Japanese Marriage Institutions in the Heian Period." *Harvard Journal of Asiatic Studies* 27:103–67.

Nakane, Chie. *Japanese Society*. Berkeley: University of California Press, 1970.

Perry, Linda. "Mothers, Wives and Daughters in Osaka: Autonomy, Alliance and Professionalism." Ph.D. diss., University of Pittsburgh, 1976.

Pharr, Susan. *Political Women in Japan*. Berkeley: University of California Press, 1981.

Plath, David. *The After Hours*. Berkeley: University of California Press, 1964.

Reischauer, Edwin. *Tradition and Transformation*. New York: Houghton Mifflin, 1973.

Robins-Mowry, Dorothy. *The Hidden Sun: Women of Modern Japan*. Boulder: Westview Press, 1983.

Rohlen, Thomas. *For Harmony and Strength: Japanese White Collar Organization in Anthropological Perspective*. Berkeley: University of California Press, 1974.

———. *Japan's High Schools*. Berkeley: University of California Press, 1983.

Seidensticker, Edward, trans. *The Gossamer Years (Kagero Nikki)*. Tokyo: Charles Tuttle, 1964.

Sievers, Sharon. *Flowers in Salt*. Stanford: Stanford University Press, 1983.

Statistics Bureau, Japan. *Statistical Handbook of Japan, 1986*. Tokyo: Management and Coordination Agency, 1986.

Suzuki, Takao. "Language and Behavior in Japan: The Conceptualization of Personal Relations." *Japan Quarterly* 23, 3 (1976): 255–66.

Taeuber, Irene. *The Population of Japan*. Princeton: Princeton University Press, 1958.

Terkel, Studs. *Working*. New York: Pantheon Books, 1972.

Walker, Charles, and Robert Guest. *The Man on the Assembly Line*. New Haven: Institute of Human Relations, Yale University, 1952.

Weil, Simone. "Factory Work." In *The Simone Weil Reader*, ed. George Panichas. Moyer Bell, 1977.

White, Merry. *The Japanese Educational Challenge*. New York: Free Press, 1986.

White, Merry, and Barbara Molony. *Proceedings of the Tokyo Symposium on Women*. Tokyo: International Group for the Study of Women, 1978.

Yoshida Noboru and Kanda Michiko, eds. *Gendai josei no ishiki to seikatsu* (The consciousness and life of contemporary women). Tokyo: NHK Books, 1975.

INDEX

JEANNIE LO spent two years researching the lives and conditions of contemporary Japanese women working in the offices and assembly lines at Brother Industries in Nagoya, Japan. In 1988, Ms. Lo received her B.A. in East Asian Studies from Harvard University, where her research thesis, on which this book is based, won an award of summa cum laude, as well as the university's Hoopes Prize for outstanding work by a senior. She is presently a copy editor at Look Japan, Ltd. in Tokyo.